D1093766

IN THE KITCHEN WITH
ALAIN PASSARD

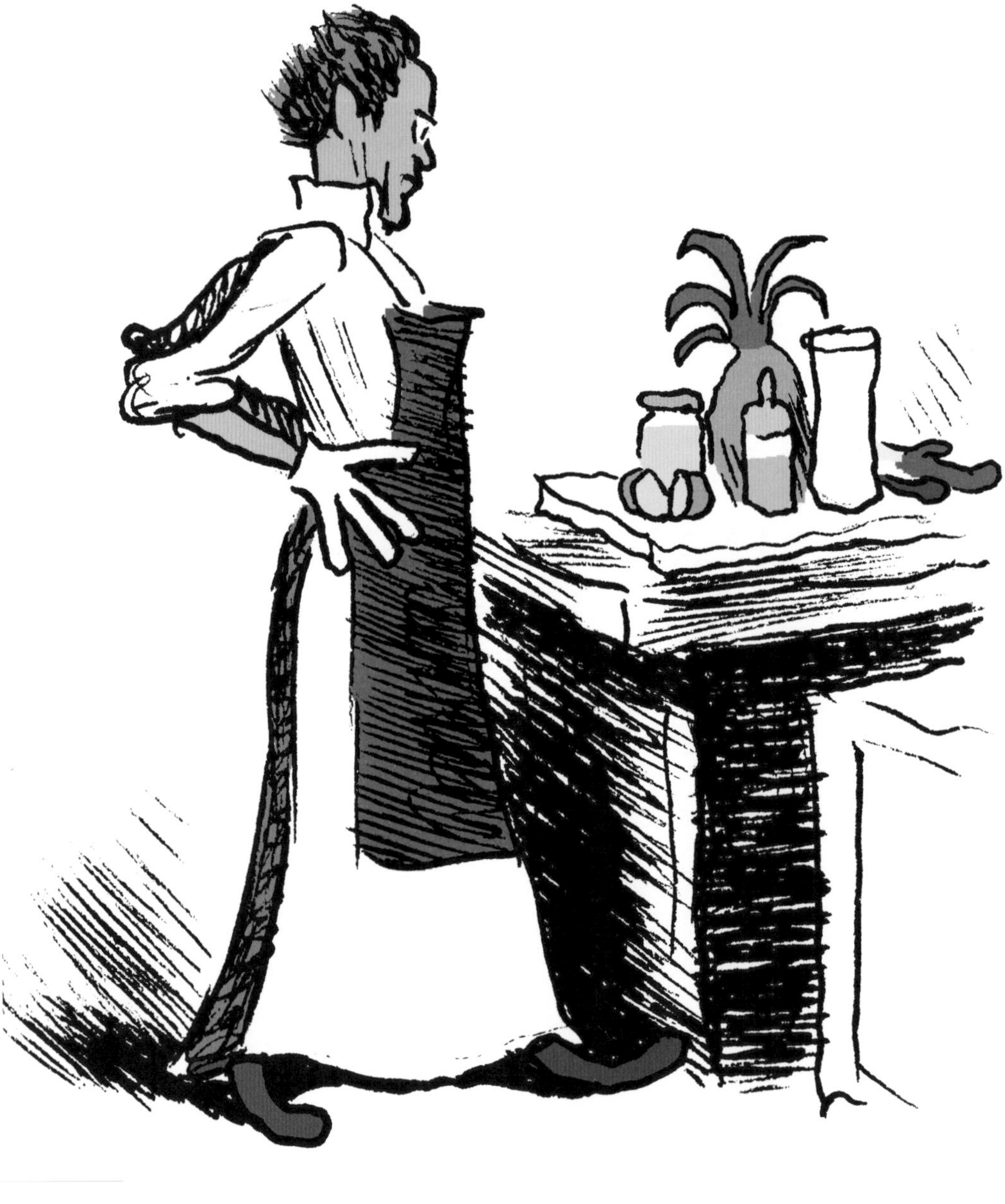

IN THE KITCHEN WITH

ALAIN PASSARD

Inside the World (and Mind) of a Master Chef

Written and illustrated by
CHRISTOPHE BLAIN

Recipes by
ALAIN PASSARD

With inking by
CLÉMENCE SAPIN & CHRISTOPHE BLAIN

Graphic concept by
NÉJIB BELHADJ KACEM

CHRONICLE BOOKS
SAN FRANCISCO

First published in the United States of America in 2013 by Chronicle Books LLC.
First published in France in 2011 by Gallimard.

Copyright © 2011 by Gallimard.
All rights reserved. No part of this book may be reproduced
in any form without written permission from the publisher.

Library of Congress Cataloging-in-Publication Data available.

ISBN 978-1-4521-1346-3

Manufactured in China

Text and illustrations by Christophe Blain
Translation by Elizabeth Bell

10 9 8 7 6 5 4 3 2

Chronicle Books LLC
680 Second Street
San Francisco, California 94107
www.chroniclebooks.com

The chef thanks his team.

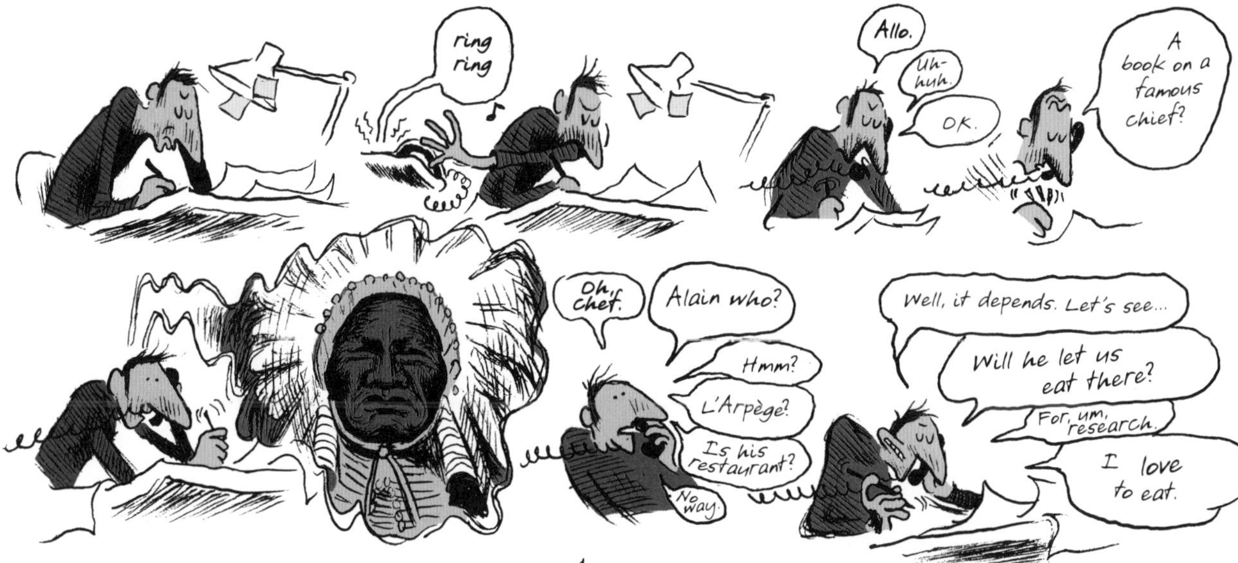

ring ring
Allo.
Uh-huh.
OK.
A book on a famous chief?
Oh, chef.
Alain who?
Hmm?
L'Arpège?
Is his restaurant?
No way.
Well, it depends. Let's see...
Will he let us eat there?
For, um, research.
I love to eat.

IN THE KITCHEN WITH ALAIN PASSARD

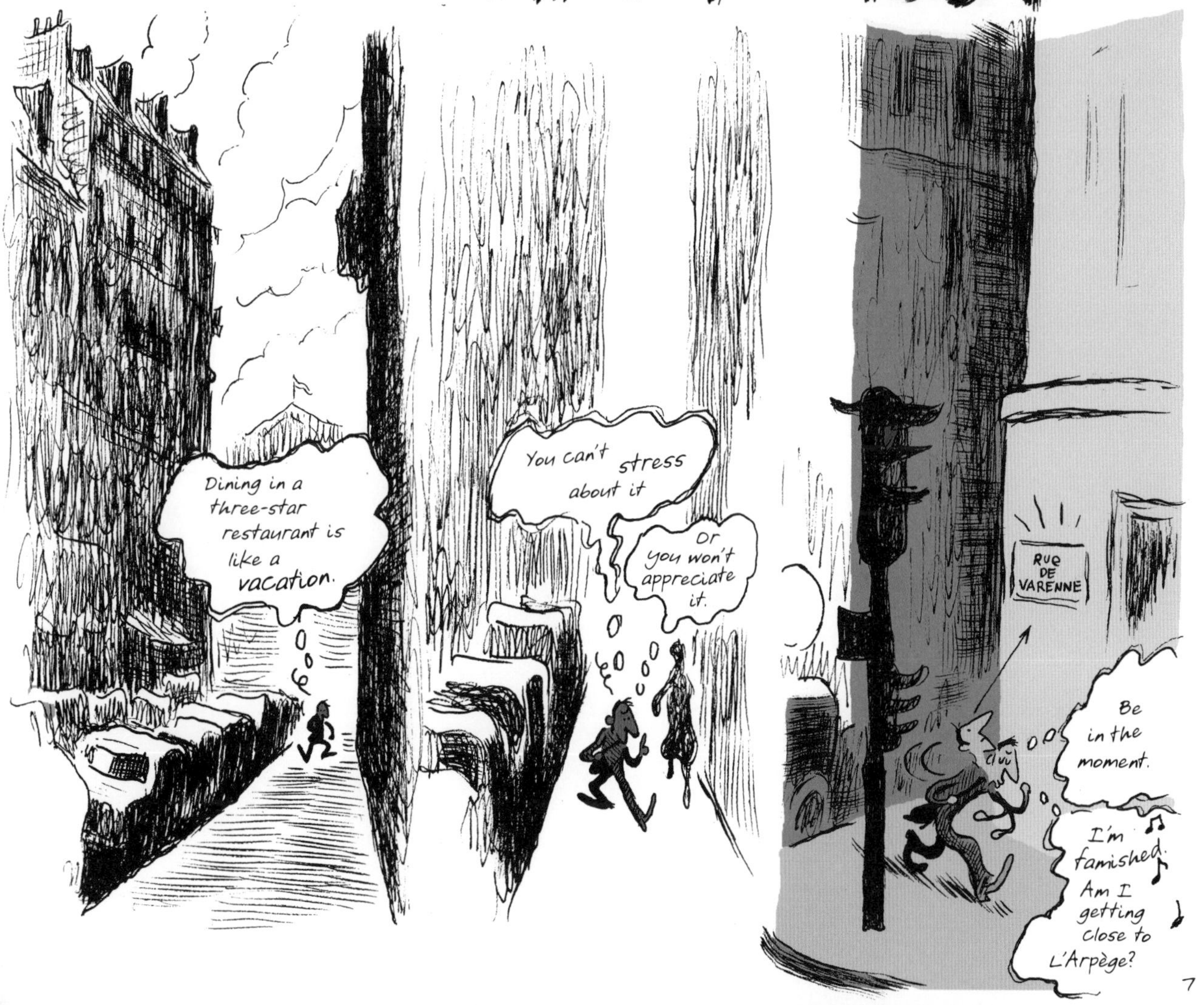

Dining in a three-star restaurant is like a vacation.
You can't stress about it
Or you won't appreciate it.
RUE DE VARENNE
Be in the moment.
I'm famished. Am I getting close to L'Arpège?

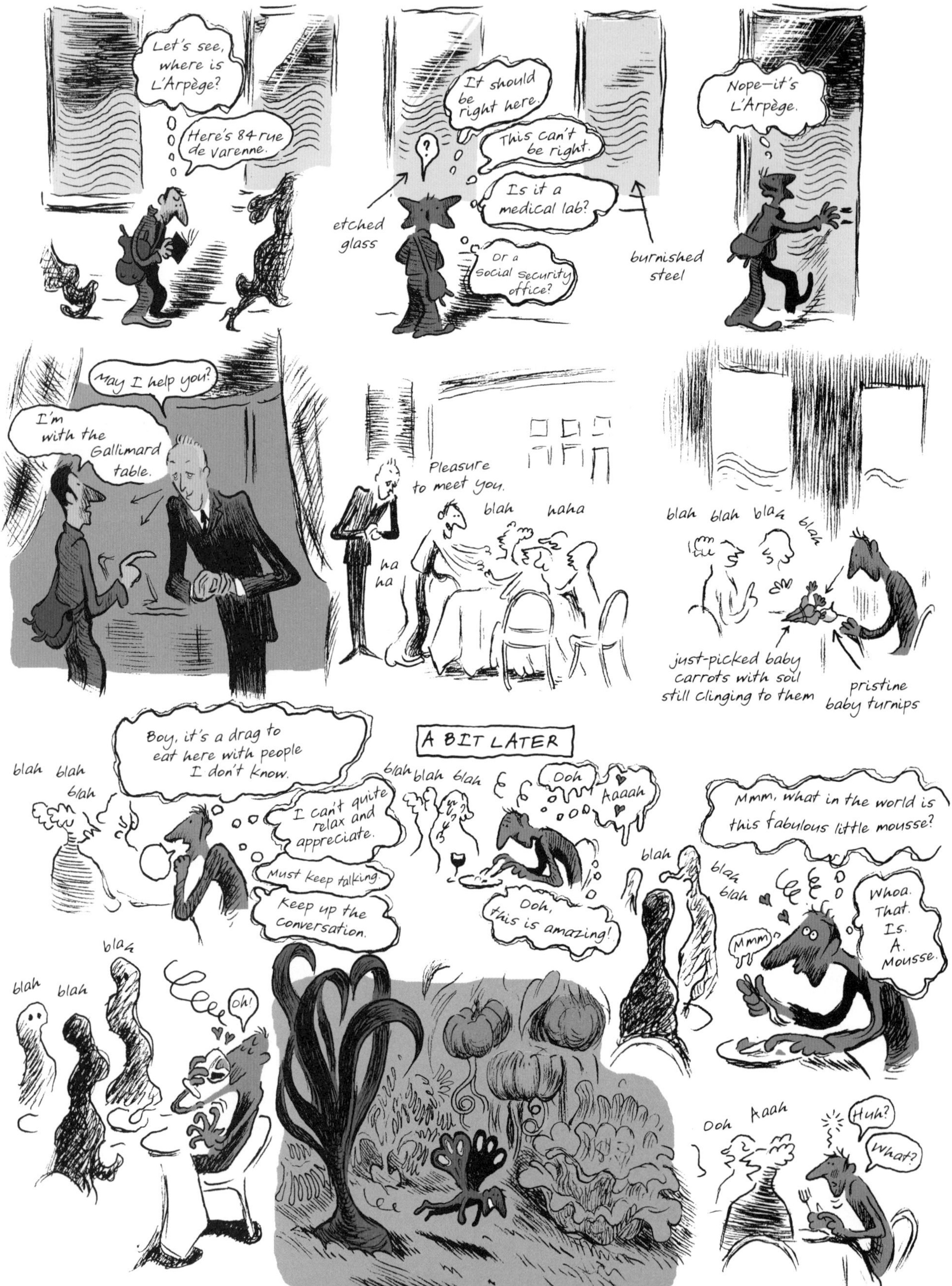
Let's see, where is L'Arpège?
Here's 84 rue de Varenne.
It should be right here.
This can't be right.
Is it a medical lab?
Or a social security office?
etched glass
burnished steel
Nope—it's L'Arpège.
May I help you?
I'm with the Gallimard table.
Pleasure to meet you.
blah
haha
ha ha
blah blah blah blah
just-picked baby carrots with soil still clinging to them
pristine baby turnips
A BIT LATER
Boy, it's a drag to eat here with people I don't know.
blah blah blah
I can't quite relax and appreciate.
Must keep talking.
Keep up the conversation.
blah blah blah
Ooh
Aaaah
Ooh, this is amazing!
Mmm, what in the world is this fabulous little mousse?
blah
blah blah
Mmm
Whoa. That. Is. A. Mousse.
blah blah blah
Oh!
Ooh Aaah
Huh?
What?

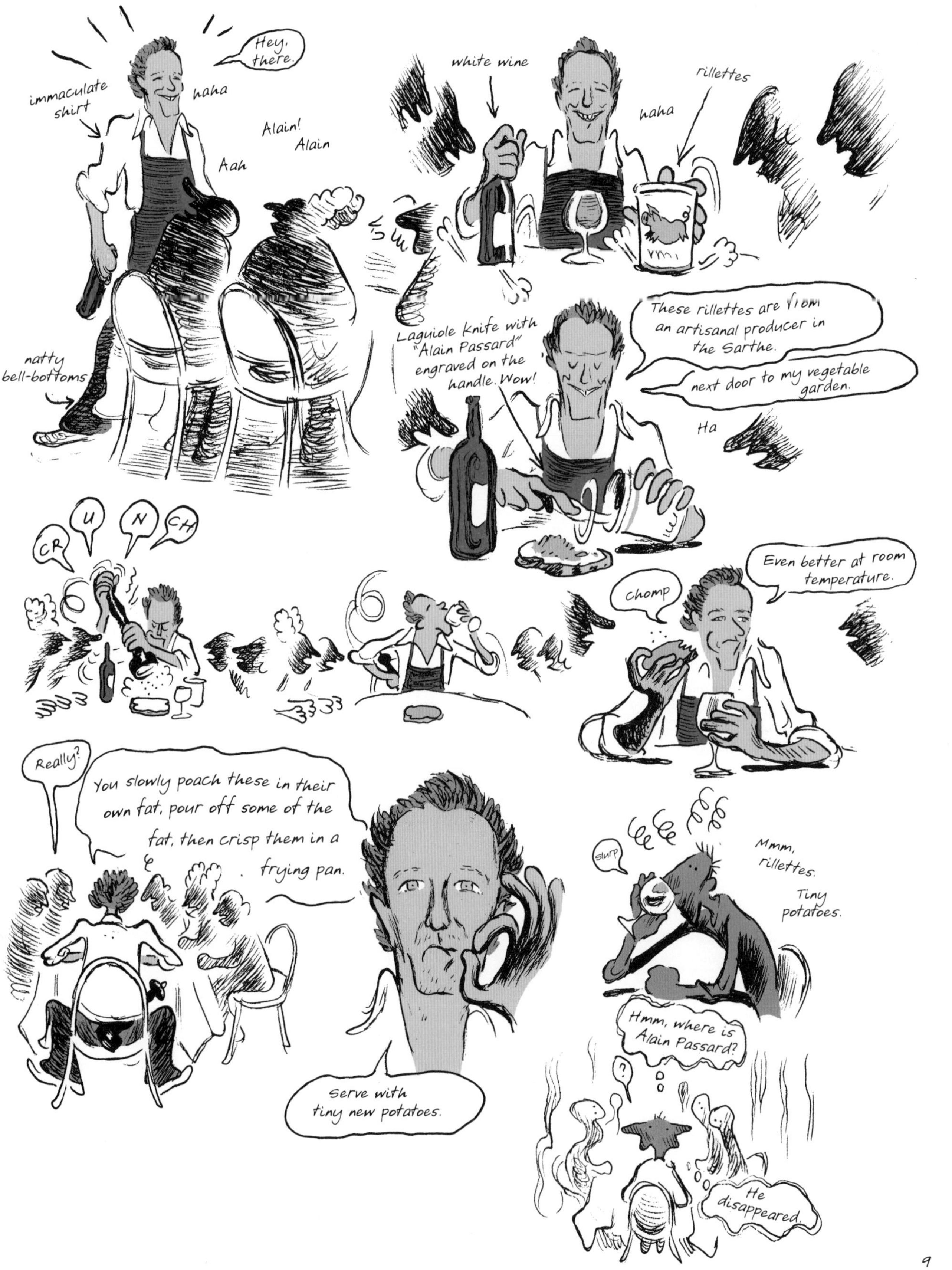

Hey, there.
immaculate shirt
haha
Alain! Alain
Aah
natty bell-bottoms
white wine
haha
rillettes
Laguiole knife with "Alain Passard" engraved on the handle. Wow!
These rillettes are from an artisanal producer in the Sarthe.
next door to my vegetable garden.
Ha
CR
U
N
CH
chomp
Even better at room temperature.
Really?
You slowly poach these in their own fat, pour off some of the fat, then crisp them in a frying pan.
Serve with tiny new potatoes.
slurp
Mmm, rillettes.
Tiny potatoes.
Hmm, where is Alain Passard?
?
He disappeared.

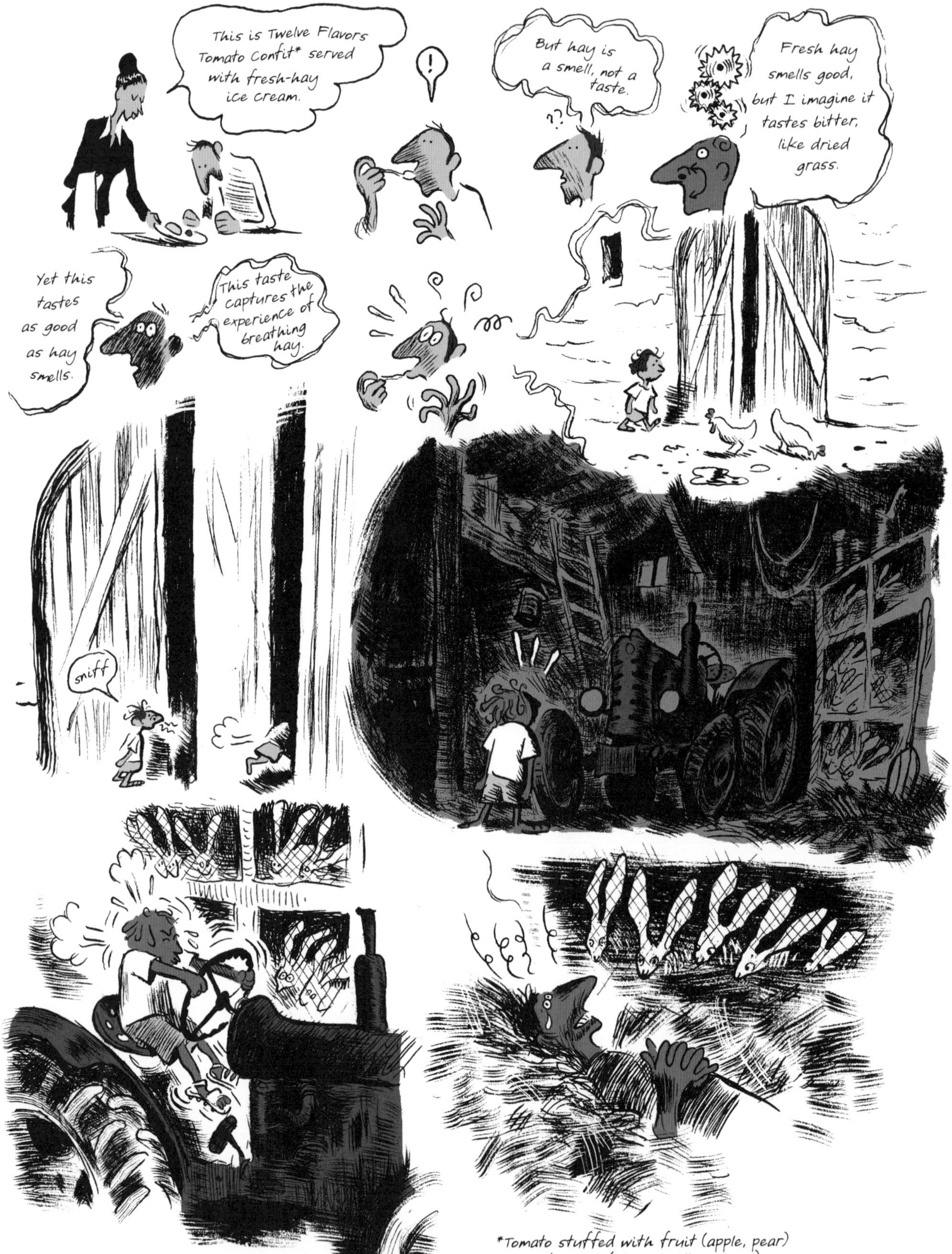

This is Twelve Flavors Tomato Confit* served with fresh-hay ice cream.
!
But hay is a smell, not a taste.
??
Fresh hay smells good, but I imagine it tastes bitter, like dried grass.
Yet this tastes as good as hay smells.
This taste captures the experience of breathing hay.
sniff

*Tomato stuffed with fruit (apple, pear) and spices (clove, vanilla, ginger)

"Green Caviar" Petits Pois
with Pink Grapefruit and Fresh Mint

∎∎◣∎◢∎∎∎

Heart of Baby Cabbage
and Parmesan Slaw

"Green Caviar" Petits Pois with Pink Grapefruit and Fresh Mint

SERVES 4

In a large sauté pan over low heat, melt 1 tablespoon of salted butter with 4 teaspoons of tiny fresh petits pois; 4 spring shallots, chopped fine; and 1 clove of garlic, crushed. The size of the sauté pan is important: the peas should cover the bottom, but shouldn't be piled on top of each other. When you stir, you should see the bottom of the pan. Add ¼ cup of water, cover with parchment paper to preserve the aromas, and allow to simmer and steam for 4 to 6 minutes, depending on the size of the peas.

Season with a pinch of fleur de sel. Serve in four warm soup bowls. Divide among the bowls a freshly peeled, pitted, and thinly sliced grapefruit. Add 4 leaves of fresh mint or lemon balm, chopped fine.

In this recipe, the idea is to warm the tiny petits pois, not to cook them! For larger peas, add a little more water and cook a bit longer.

Called "green caviar" because tiny petits pois are the size of sturgeon eggs, and just as tender!

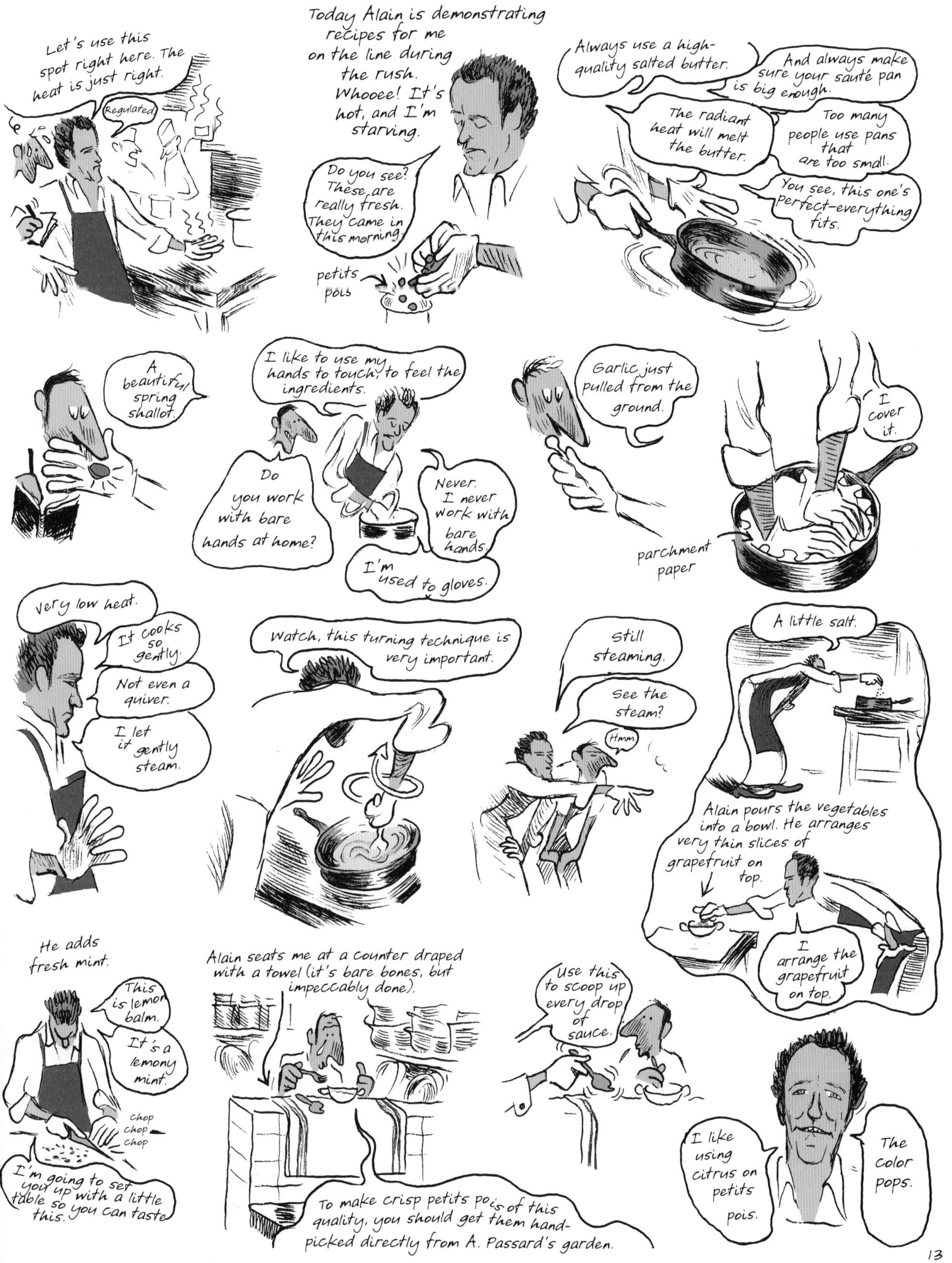

Let's use this spot right here. The heat is just right.
Regulated
Today Alain is demonstrating recipes for me on the line during the rush. Whooee! It's hot, and I'm starving.
Do you see? These are really fresh. They came in this morning.
petits pois
Always use a high-quality salted butter.
And always make sure your sauté pan is big enough.
The radiant heat will melt the butter.
Too many people use pans that are too small.
You see, this one's perfect—everything fits.
A beautiful spring shallot.
I like to use my hands to touch, to feel the ingredients.
Do you work with bare hands at home?
Never. I never work with bare hands.
I'm used to gloves.
Garlic just pulled from the ground.
I cover it.
parchment paper
Very low heat.
It cooks so gently.
Not even a quiver.
I let it gently steam.
Watch, this turning technique is very important.
Still steaming.
See the steam?
Hmm.
A little salt.
Alain pours the vegetables into a bowl. He arranges very thin slices of grapefruit on top.
I arrange the grapefruit on top.
He adds fresh mint.
This is lemon balm.
It's a lemony mint.
Chop chop chop
I'm going to set you up with a little table so you can taste this.
Alain seats me at a counter draped with a towel (it's bare bones, but impeccably done).
Use this to scoop up every drop of sauce.
To make crisp petits pois of this quality, you should get them hand-picked directly from A. Passard's garden.
I like using citrus on petits pois.
The color pops.

Heart of Baby Cabbage and Parmesan Slaw

SERVES 4

Using a mandoline, grate a young loose-leaf cabbage, such as baby bok choy, very finely into a large bowl. You will get a sort of raw sauerkraut. Untangle the shreds and add 1 young carrot, freshly grated; 1 bunch of small red radishes, quartered; 4 small white or black radishes, sliced on a mandoline into thin rounds; and the crushed leaves of ½ bundle of tarragon. Dress with a good spritz of olive oil, 3 to 4 tablespoons of sweetened soy sauce, and 2 tablespoons of grated Parmesan. *Voilà*—that's it! Serve with grilled country bread, rubbed with lemon peel.

The Parmesan and soy sauce provide enough salt for this cabbage salad.

Tarragon has an aniselike flavor, which adds freshness and fullness.

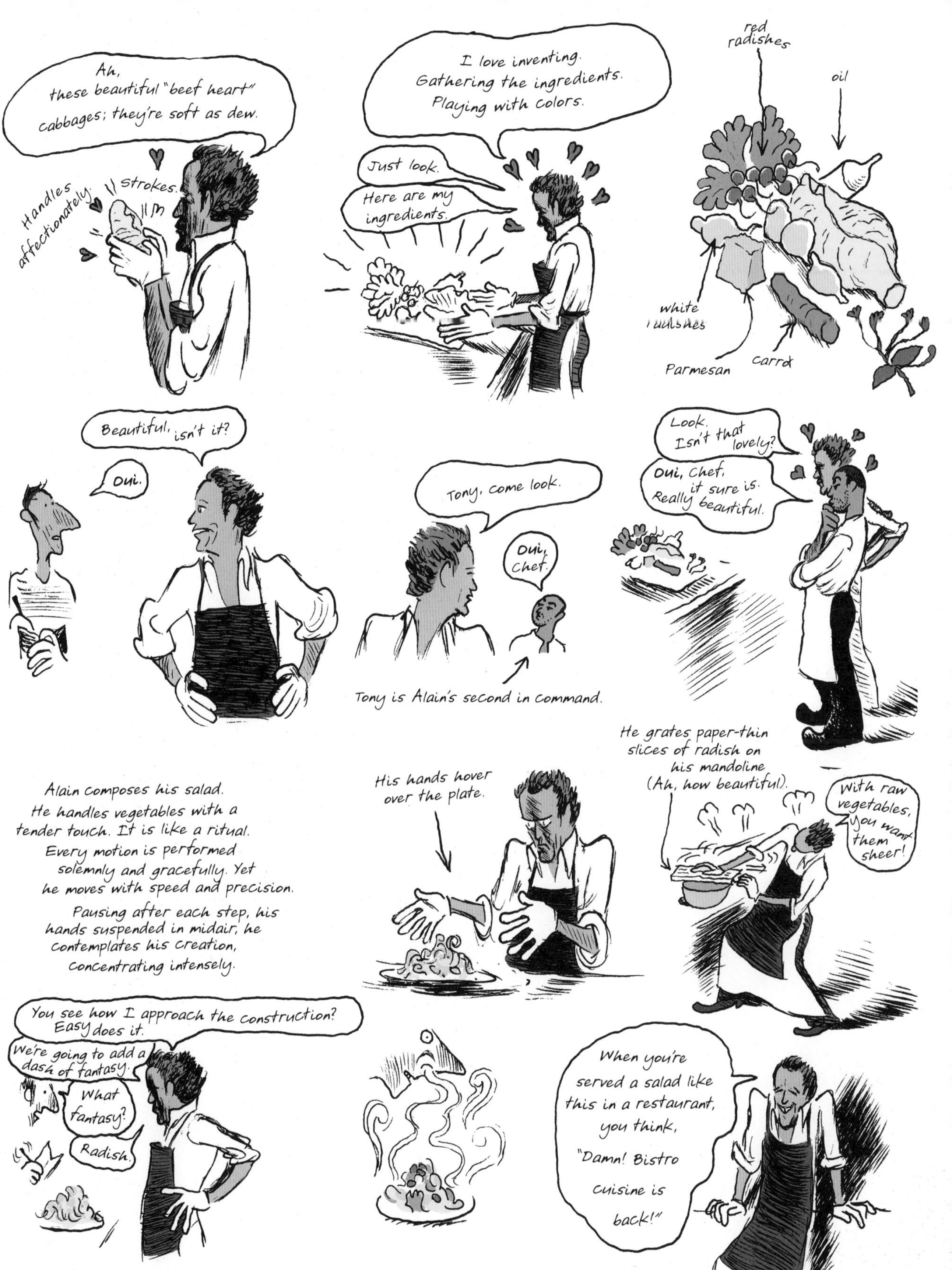

Ah, these beautiful "beef heart" cabbages; they're soft as dew.
Handles affectionately.
Strokes.
I love inventing. Gathering the ingredients. Playing with colors.
Just look.
Here are my ingredients.
red radishes
oil
white
Parmesan
carrot
Beautiful, isn't it?
Oui.
Tony, come look.
Oui, Chef.
Tony is Alain's second in command.
Look. Isn't that lovely?
Oui, Chef, it sure is. Really beautiful.
Alain composes his salad. He handles vegetables with a tender touch. It is like a ritual. Every motion is performed solemnly and gracefully. Yet he moves with speed and precision.
Pausing after each step, his hands suspended in midair, he contemplates his creation, concentrating intensely.
His hands hover over the plate.
He grates paper-thin slices of radish on his mandoline (Ah, how beautiful).
With raw vegetables, you want them sheer!
You see how I approach the construction? Easy does it.
We're going to add a dash of fantasy.
What fantasy?
Radish.
When you're served a salad like this in a restaurant, you think, "Damn! Bistro cuisine is back!"

IN THE KITCHEN

The lunch service is about to begin. I've wedged myself into a corner because the kitchen is tiny.

The atmosphere is relaxed.

The cooks are doing their prep work. They clean and peel vegetables. (Sometimes Alain pitches in a little, warming up for service.)

There's even a customer who has paid to apprentice in the kitchen before his lunch. He's peeling.

FLAP FLAP

Tony, make me some carrot oil.

Oui, Chef.

What do we have to play with today?

We have radishes, Chef.

Make me some radish oil.

Very black.

We're very into oils right now.

We mix oil with a ground vegetable,

and the flavor of the vegetable infuses the oil.

We don't want a heavy sauce, so use a fresh oil.

But not olive oil—it's too dominant.

We use a beautiful pale peanut oil.

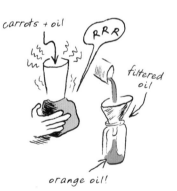

carrots + oil

RRR

filtered oil

orange oil!

Make me some cauliflower bread crumbs.

Oui, Chef.

Ha ha! Watch this. I use these like bread crumbs.

Grate the cauliflower, but keep the florets.

The florets are very tender.

Tony, will you make me a little *crème anglaise*?

Oui, Chef.

One club in, no restrictions. Must leave at 2:45 on the dot.

FLAP

Order in.

A "club" is a formal lunch. "No restrictions" means "no dietary restrictions." Customers don't hesitate to tell us what they can't or won't eat, which is passed to the kitchen via routing slips that might look like: "M. CALICO, 12:30, wife is vegan, no eggs, no animal fat, no butter. **Monsieur** eats everything!" Some regulars like to keep up their diets here. They ask the chef to eliminate this or that ingredient.

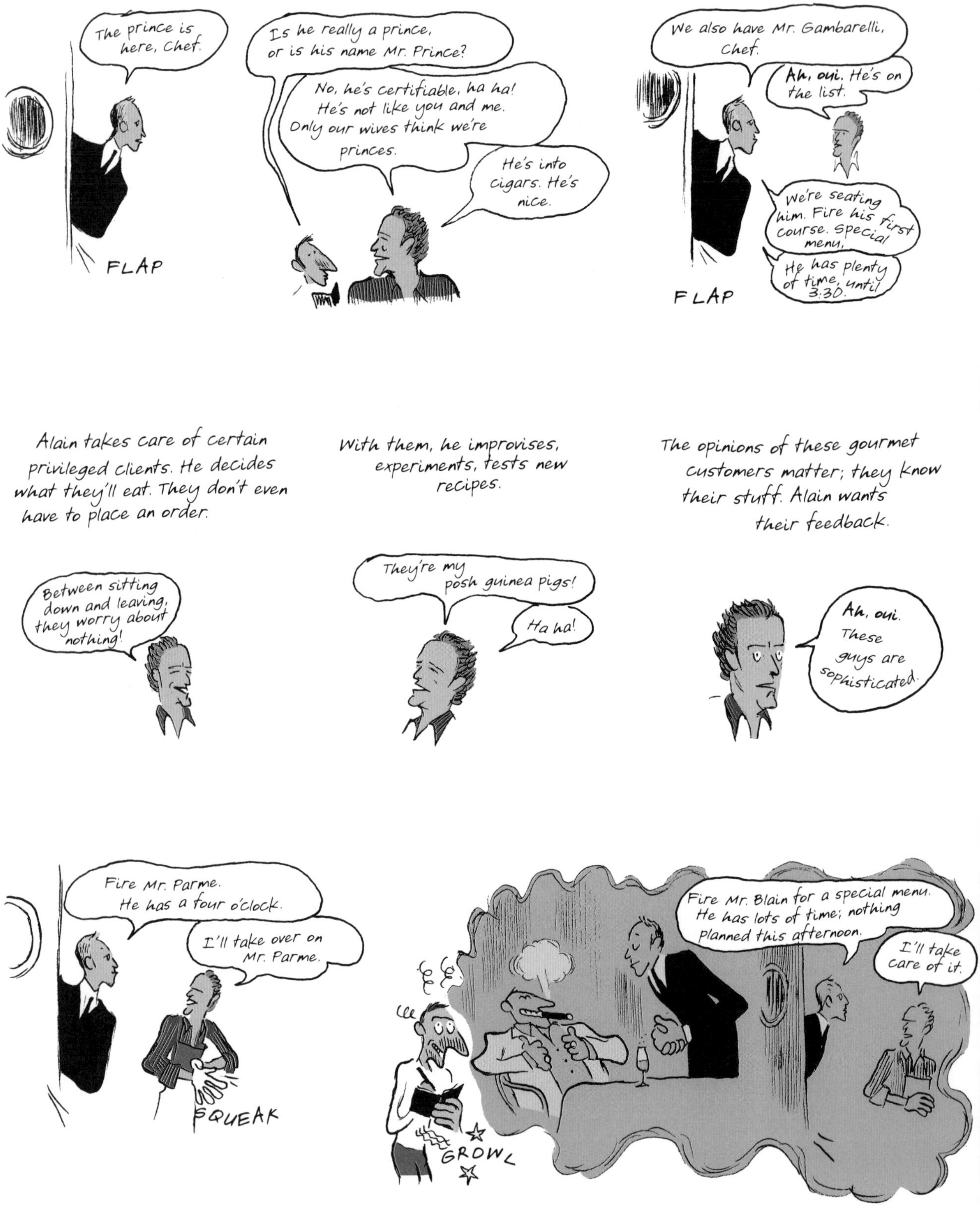
The prince is here, Chef.
FLAP
Is he really a prince, or is his name Mr. Prince?
No, he's certifiable, ha ha! He's not like you and me. Only our wives think we're princes.
He's into cigars. He's nice.
We also have Mr. Gambarelli, Chef.
Ah, oui. He's on the list.
We're seating him. Fire his first course. Special menu.
He has plenty of time, until 3:30.
FLAP
Alain takes care of certain privileged clients. He decides what they'll eat. They don't even have to place an order.
Between sitting down and leaving, they worry about nothing!
With them, he improvises, experiments, tests new recipes.
They're my posh guinea pigs!
Ha ha!
The opinions of these gourmet customers matter; they know their stuff. Alain wants their feedback.
Ah, oui. These guys are sophisticated.
Fire Mr. Parme. He has a four o'clock.
I'll take over on Mr. Parme.
SQUEAK
Fire Mr. Blain for a special menu. He has lots of time; nothing planned this afternoon.
I'll take care of it.
GROWL

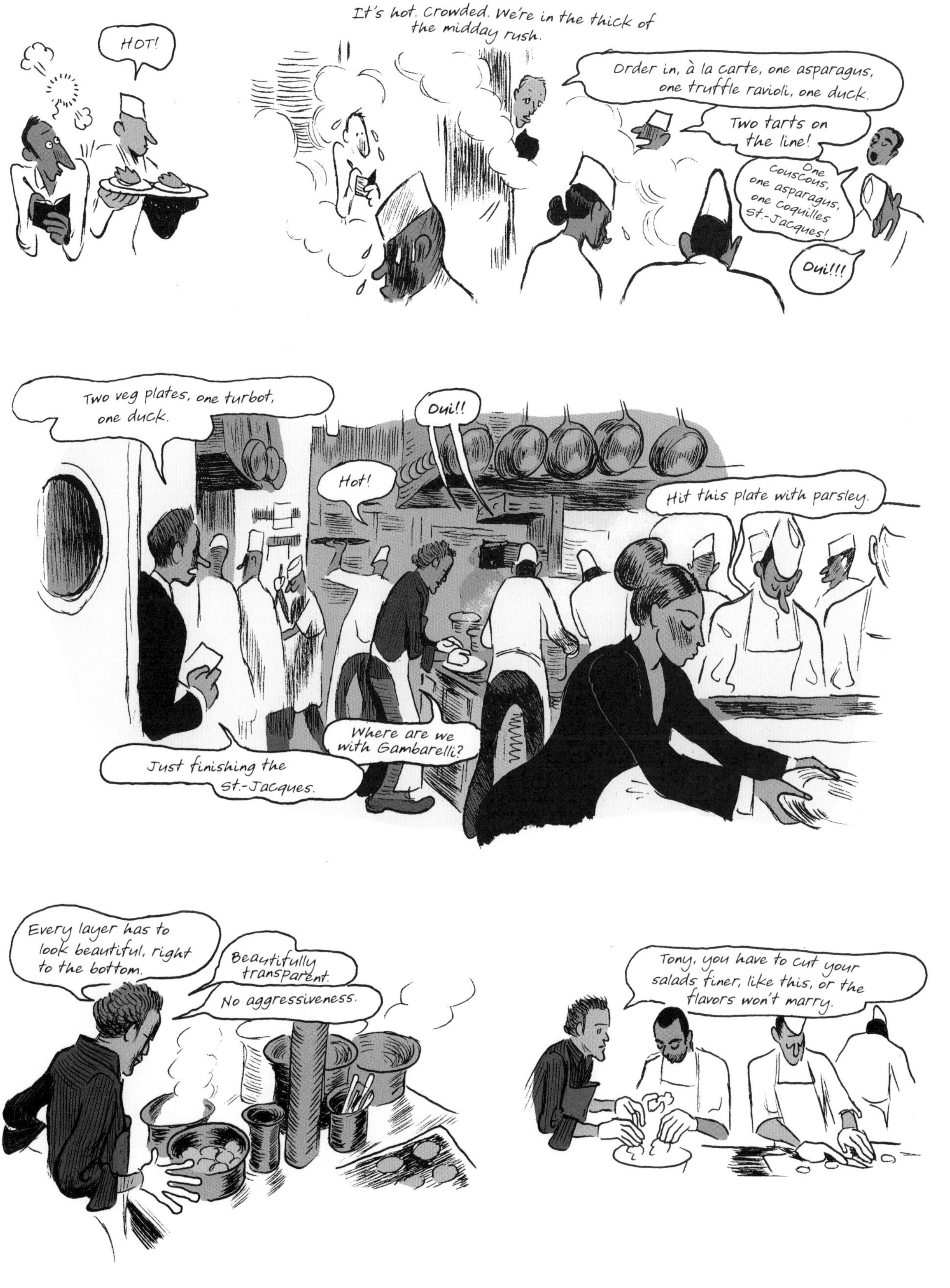
HOT!
It's hot. Crowded. We're in the thick of the midday rush.
Order in, à la carte, one asparagus, one truffle ravioli, one duck.
Two tarts on the line!
One couscous, one asparagus, one coquilles St.-Jacques!
Oui!!!
Two veg plates, one turbot, one duck.
Oui!!
Hot!
Hit this plate with parsley.
Where are we with Gambarelli?
Just finishing the St.-Jacques.
Every layer has to look beautiful, right to the bottom.
Beautifully transparent.
No aggressiveness.
Tony, you have to cut your salads finer, like this, or the flavors won't marry.

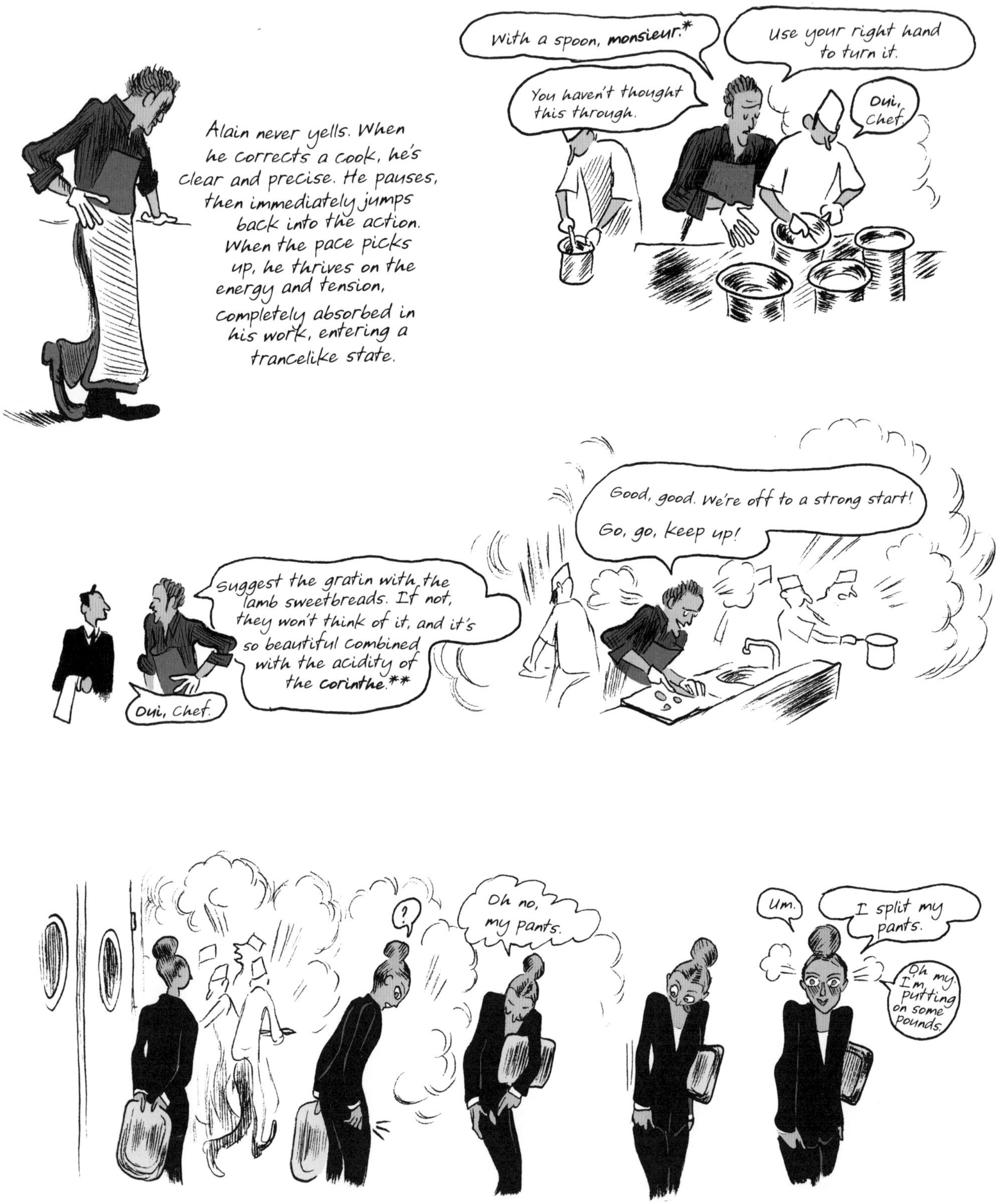

Alain never yells. When he corrects a cook, he's clear and precise. He pauses, then immediately jumps back into the action. When the pace picks up, he thrives on the energy and tension, completely absorbed in his work, entering a trancelike state.
With a spoon, **monsieur.***
You haven't thought this through.
Use your right hand to turn it.
Oui, Chef.
Suggest the gratin with the lamb sweetbreads. If not, they won't think of it, and it's so beautiful combined with the acidity of the **corinthe.****
Oui, Chef.
Good, good. We're off to a strong start!
Go, go, keep up!
?
Oh no, my pants.
Um.
I split my pants.
Oh my. I'm putting on some pounds.

* In the kitchen, everyone is addressed using courtesy titles.

** A sauce made of white wine and currants.

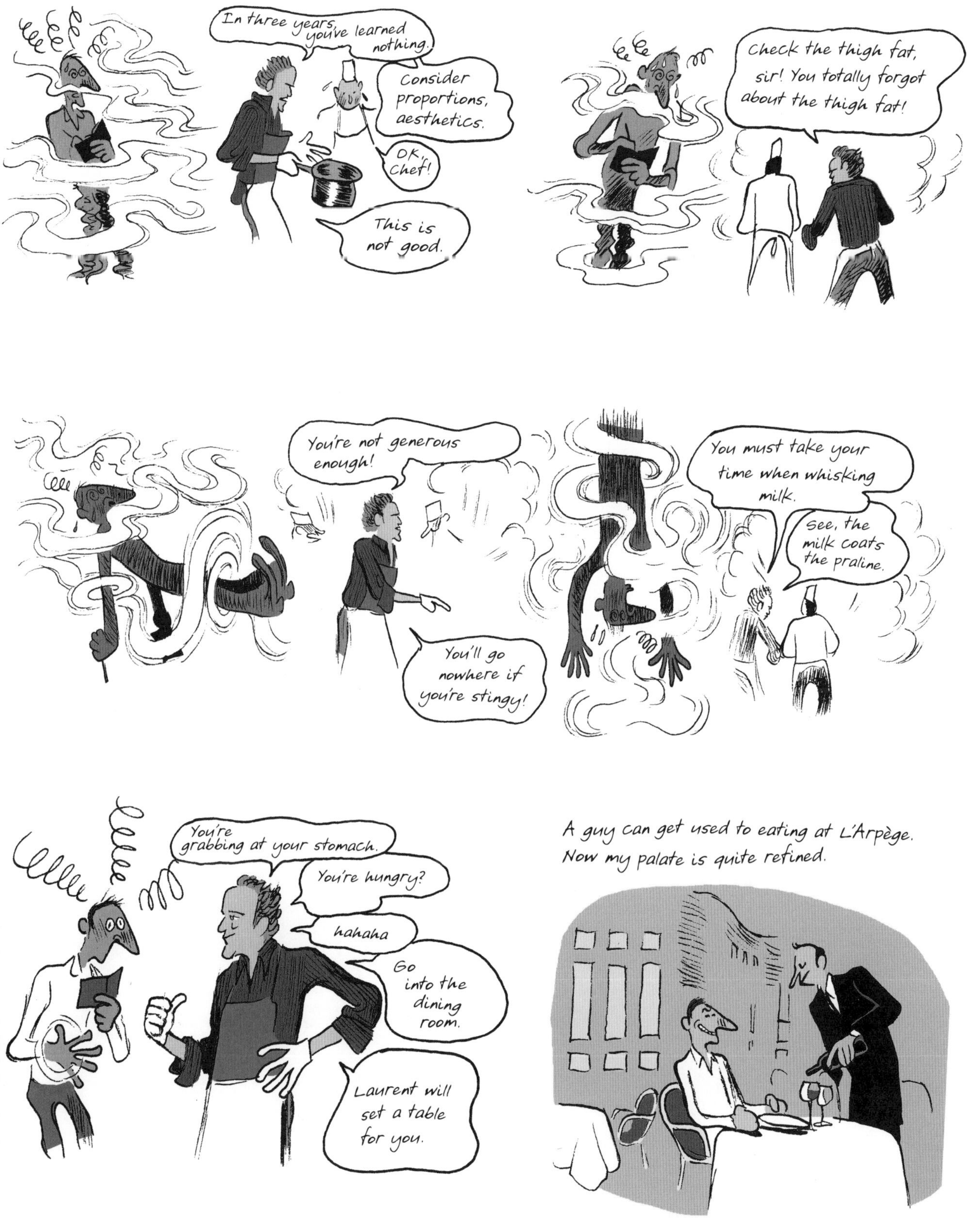
In three years, you've learned nothing.
Consider proportions, aesthetics.
OK, Chef!
This is not good.
Check the thigh fat, sir! You totally forgot about the thigh fat!
You're not generous enough!
You'll go nowhere if you're stingy!
You must take your time when whisking milk.
See, the milk coats the praline.
You're grabbing at your stomach.
You're hungry?
hahaha
Go into the dining room.
Laurent will set a table for you.
A guy can get used to eating at L'Arpège.
Now my palate is quite refined.

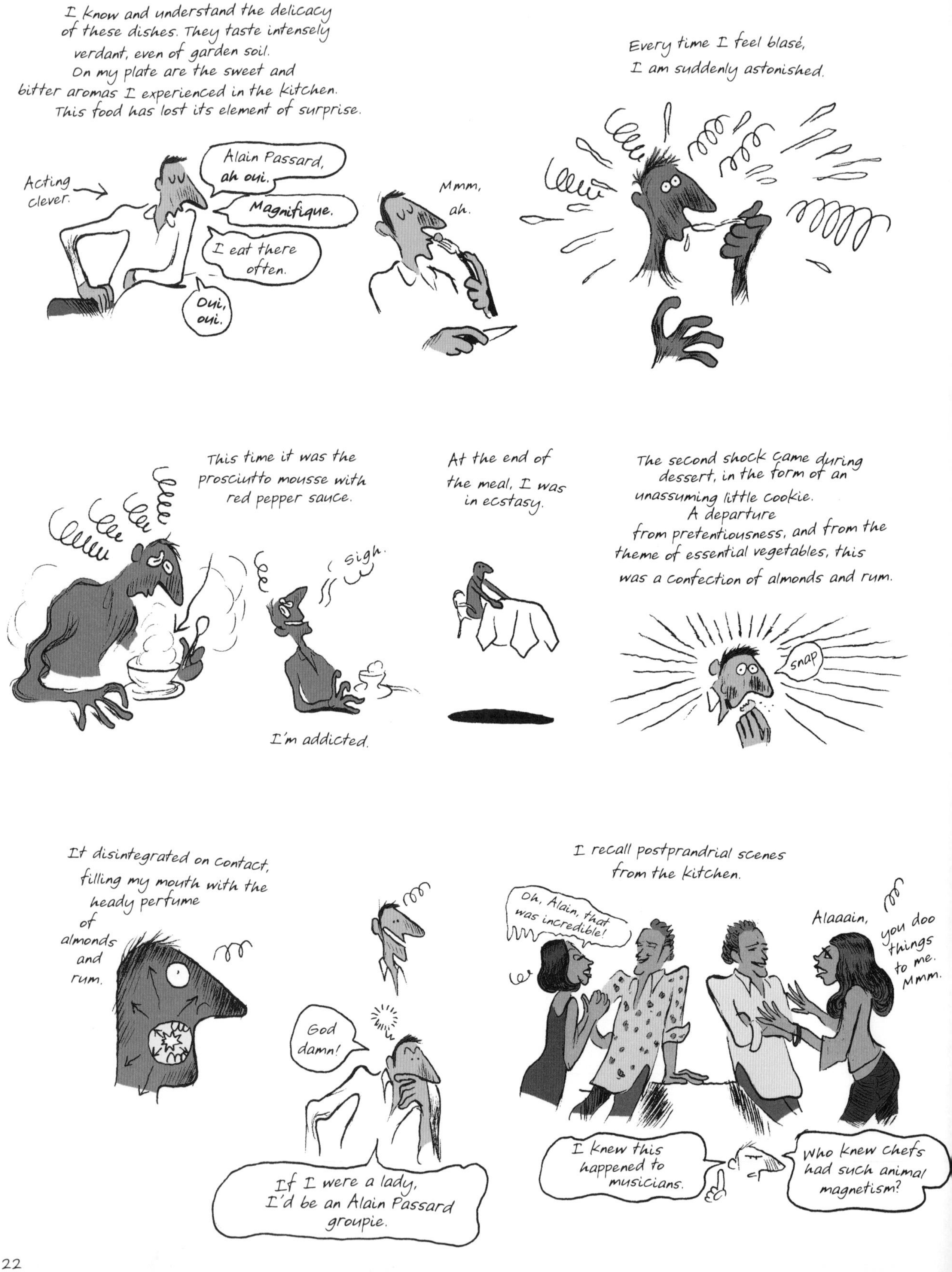

I know and understand the delicacy of these dishes. They taste intensely verdant, even of garden soil. On my plate are the sweet and bitter aromas I experienced in the kitchen. This food has lost its element of surprise.
Acting clever.
Alain Passard, ah oui.
Magnifique.
I eat there often.
Oui, oui.
Mmm, ah.
Every time I feel blasé, I am suddenly astonished.
This time it was the prosciutto mousse with red pepper sauce.
sigh.
I'm addicted.
At the end of the meal, I was in ecstasy.
The second shock came during dessert, in the form of an unassuming little cookie. A departure from pretentiousness, and from the theme of essential vegetables, this was a confection of almonds and rum.
snap
It disintegrated on contact, filling my mouth with the heady perfume of almonds and rum.
God damn!
If I were a lady, I'd be an Alain Passard groupie.
I recall postprandial scenes from the kitchen.
Oh, Alain, that was incredible!
Alaaain, you doo things to me. Mmm.
I knew this happened to musicians.
Who knew chefs had such animal magnetism?

Langoustine Carpaccio with Chives

Onion Fondue with Sorrel,
Fava Beans, and Fresh Chèvre,
with Rhubarb Chutney

Langoustine Carpaccio with Chives

SERVES 4

Wearing rubber gloves, shell 8 raw langoustines, about 3½ ounces each. On your work surface, cut each one lengthwise into three thin slices and divide the slices among four plates, filmed with olive oil. Cover each plate with plastic wrap and place another plate on top of the carpaccio, to smooth it and gently press it flat. Chill in the refrigerator. Meanwhile, finely chop a bundle of chives. Place them in a bowl and add ¾ cup of heavy cream. Remove the carpaccio from the refrigerator, take off the plastic, and encircle each serving of carpaccio with the chive cream, a dash of olive oil, fleur de sel, and freshly ground pepper. Serve with slices of freshly grilled country bread.

Before you slice each langoustine, remove the intestine with the tip of your knife.

This carpaccio is also good with a touch of lemon juice.

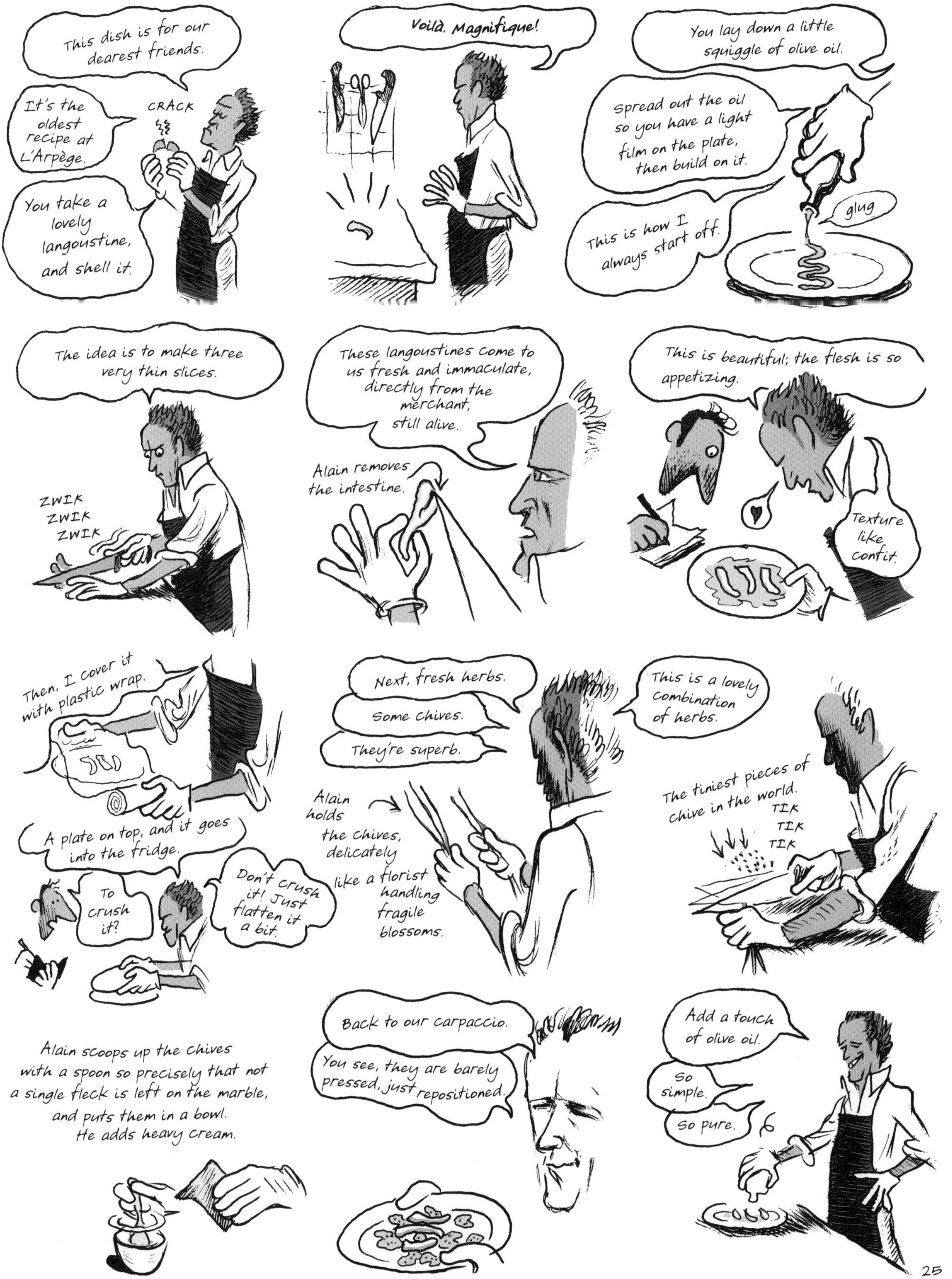
This dish is for our dearest friends.
It's the oldest recipe at L'Arpège.
CRACK
You take a lovely langoustine, and shell it.
Voilà. Magnifique!
You lay down a little squiggle of olive oil.
Spread out the oil so you have a light film on the plate, then build on it.
This is how I always start off.
glug
The idea is to make three very thin slices.
ZWIK ZWIK ZWIK
These langoustines come to us fresh and immaculate, directly from the merchant, still alive.
Alain removes the intestine.
This is beautiful; the flesh is so appetizing.
Texture like confit.
Then, I cover it with plastic wrap.
A plate on top, and it goes into the fridge.
To crush it?
Don't crush it! Just flatten it a bit.
Next, fresh herbs.
Some chives.
They're superb.
Alain holds the chives, delicately like a florist handling fragile blossoms.
This is a lovely combination of herbs.
The tiniest pieces of chive in the world.
TIK TIK TIK
Alain scoops up the chives with a spoon so precisely that not a single fleck is left on the marble, and puts them in a bowl. He adds heavy cream.
Back to our carpaccio.
You see, they are barely pressed, just repositioned.
Add a touch of olive oil.
So simple.
So pure.

Onion Fondue with Sorrel, Fava Beans, and Fresh Chèvre, with Rhubarb Chutney

SERVES 4

Warm your sauté pan evenly over low heat. Add 2 tablespoons of salted butter, 1 tablespoon of olive oil, and 3 large onions, thinly sliced on a mandoline. Let the onions soften for 20 minutes, without browning, stirring often. Next add 1 small bowl of peeled raw fava beans, 1 large bowl of fresh green sorrel leaves, and the juice of 1 small lemon. Let the fava beans warm and the sorrel wilt in the hot onions; this is very quick, 3 to 4 minutes. Add 2 tablespoons of sweet butter and serve immediately on a warm plate, with a small salad of raw baby spinach tossed with olive oil and topped with a few shards of dry fresh chèvre.

On the side, serve this red rhubarb chutney: Cut 2 stalks of rhubarb into ½-inch chunks. Put them in a large sauté pan, without piling them up, and add 12 cubes of sugar, 5 ounces of water, 5 ounces of white vinegar, 4 or 5 crushed hibiscus petals, and 1 tablespoon of mashed red berries, such as raspberries. Cook over low heat to soften the rhubarb, but don't stir, so the pieces will retain their shape.

Be sure to keep the heat low to obtain a delicate, light-colored blend of butter, oil, and liquid from the onion.

Get a Saint-André, a large white type of onion from the Cévennes region, if you can.

Why use lemon in an onion fondue? To echo the acidity of the sorrel.

When you shop, if you're lucky enough to find a small bunch of red sorrel, go for it! Its subtle acidity and flowery, springtime flavor will make your dish taste even more delicious. But it's hard to find.

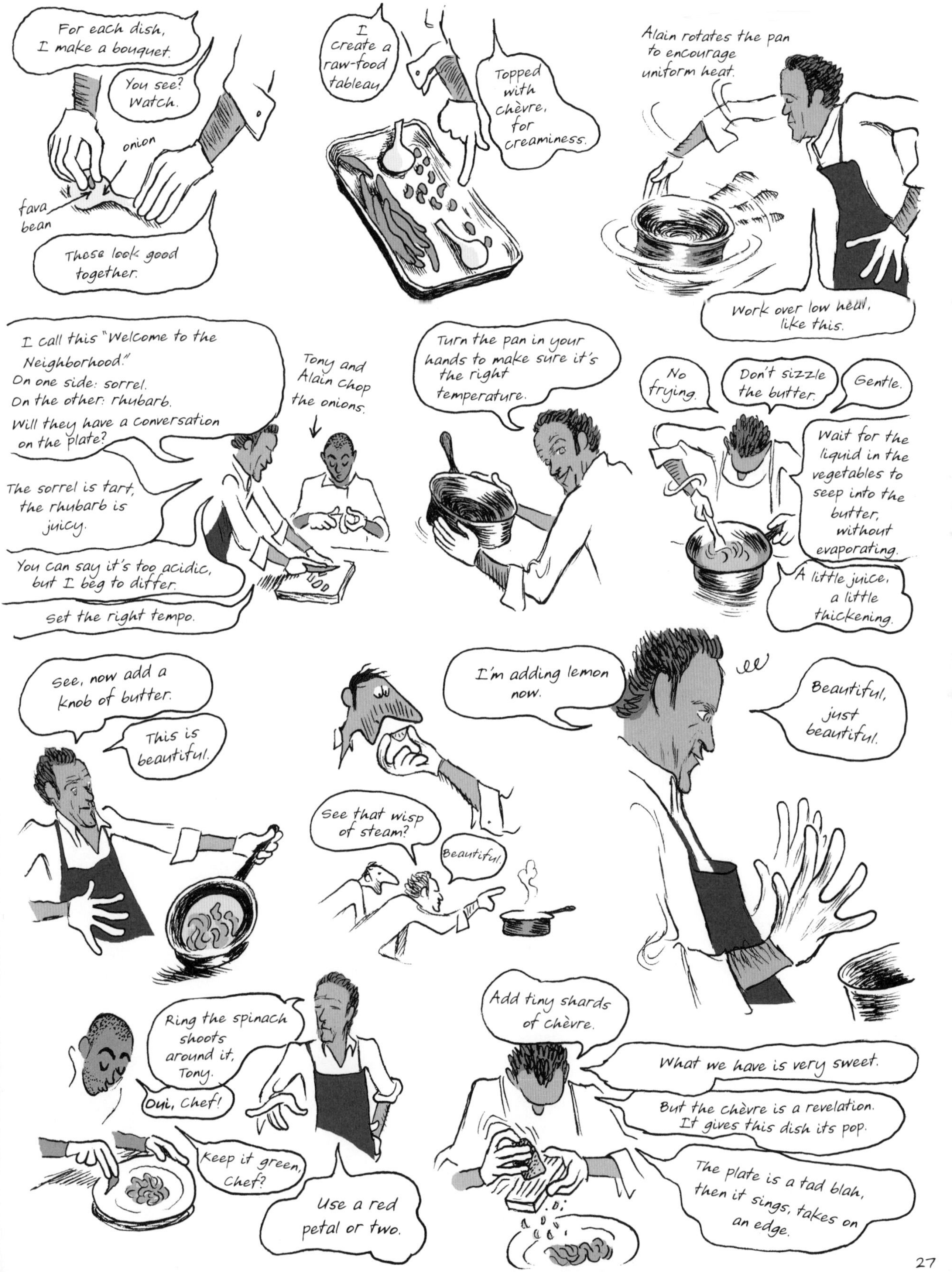

For each dish, I make a bouquet.
You see? Watch.
onion
fava bean
These look good together.
I create a raw-food tableau
Topped with chèvre, for creaminess.
Alain rotates the pan to encourage uniform heat.
Work over low heat, like this.
I call this "Welcome to the Neighborhood." On one side: sorrel. On the other: rhubarb. Will they have a conversation on the plate?
Tony and Alain chop the onions.
The sorrel is tart, the rhubarb is juicy.
You can say it's too acidic, but I beg to differ.
Set the right tempo.
Turn the pan in your hands to make sure it's the right temperature.
No frying.
Don't sizzle the butter.
Gentle.
Wait for the liquid in the vegetables to seep into the butter, without evaporating.
A little juice, a little thickening.
See, now add a knob of butter.
This is beautiful.
I'm adding lemon now.
Beautiful, just beautiful.
See that wisp of steam?
Beautiful.
Ring the spinach shoots around it, Tony.
Oui, Chef!
Keep it green, Chef?
Use a red petal or two.
Add tiny shards of chèvre.
What we have is very sweet.
But the chèvre is a revelation. It gives this dish its pop.
The plate is a tad blah, then it sings, takes on an edge.

THE AXIS OF CREATIVITY

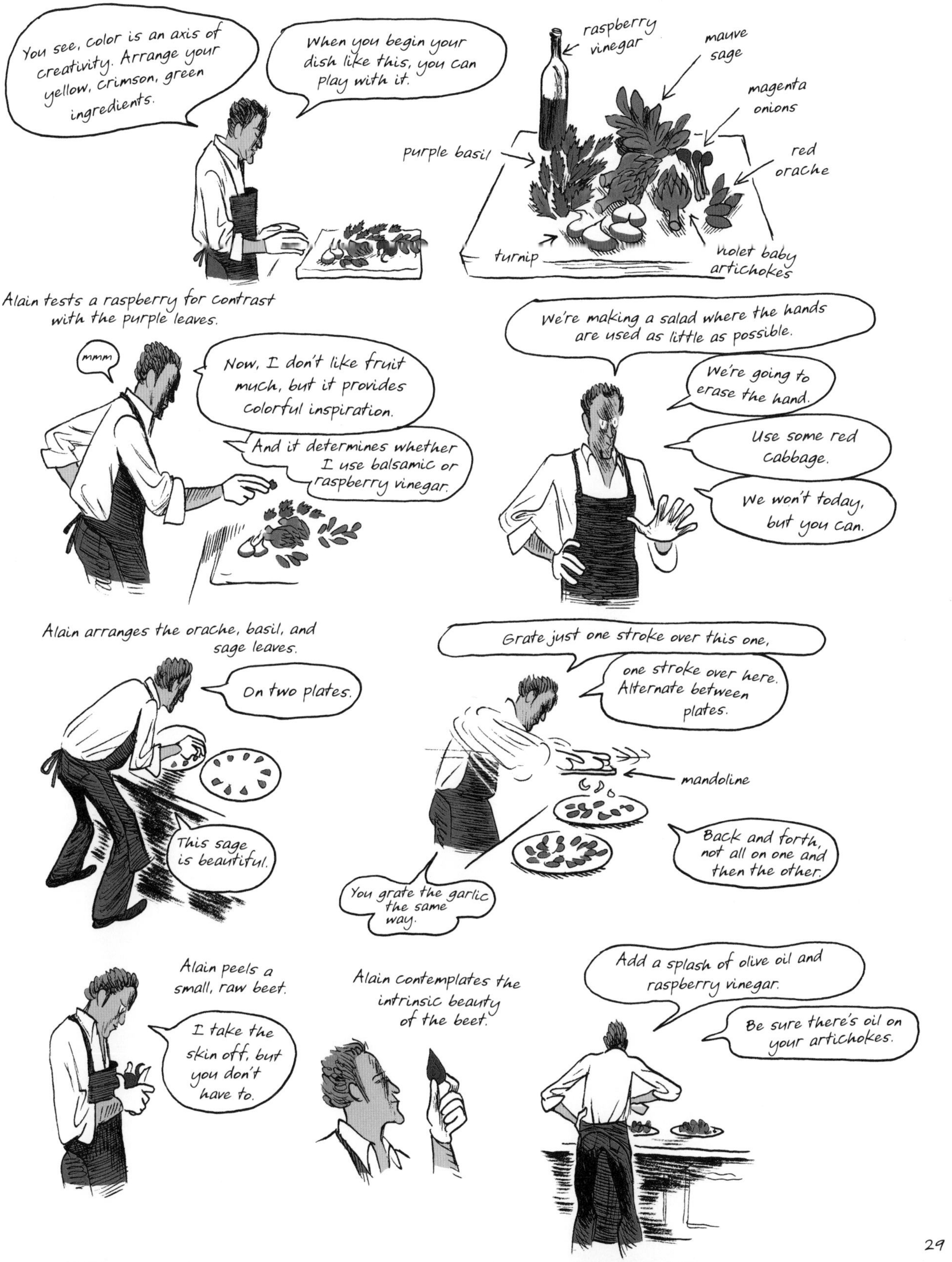

You see, color is an axis of creativity. Arrange your yellow, crimson, green ingredients.
When you begin your dish like this, you can play with it.
raspberry vinegar
mauve sage
magenta onions
purple basil
red orache
turnip
violet baby artichokes
Alain tests a raspberry for contrast with the purple leaves.
mmm
Now, I don't like fruit much, but it provides colorful inspiration.
And it determines whether I use balsamic or raspberry vinegar.
We're making a salad where the hands are used as little as possible.
We're going to erase the hand.
Use some red cabbage.
We won't today, but you can.
Alain arranges the orache, basil, and sage leaves.
On two plates.
This sage is beautiful.
Grate just one stroke over this one,
one stroke over here. Alternate between plates.
mandoline
Back and forth, not all on one and then the other.
You grate the garlic the same way.
Alain peels a small, raw beet.
I take the skin off, but you don't have to.
Alain contemplates the intrinsic beauty of the beet.
Add a splash of olive oil and raspberry vinegar.
Be sure there's oil on your artichokes.

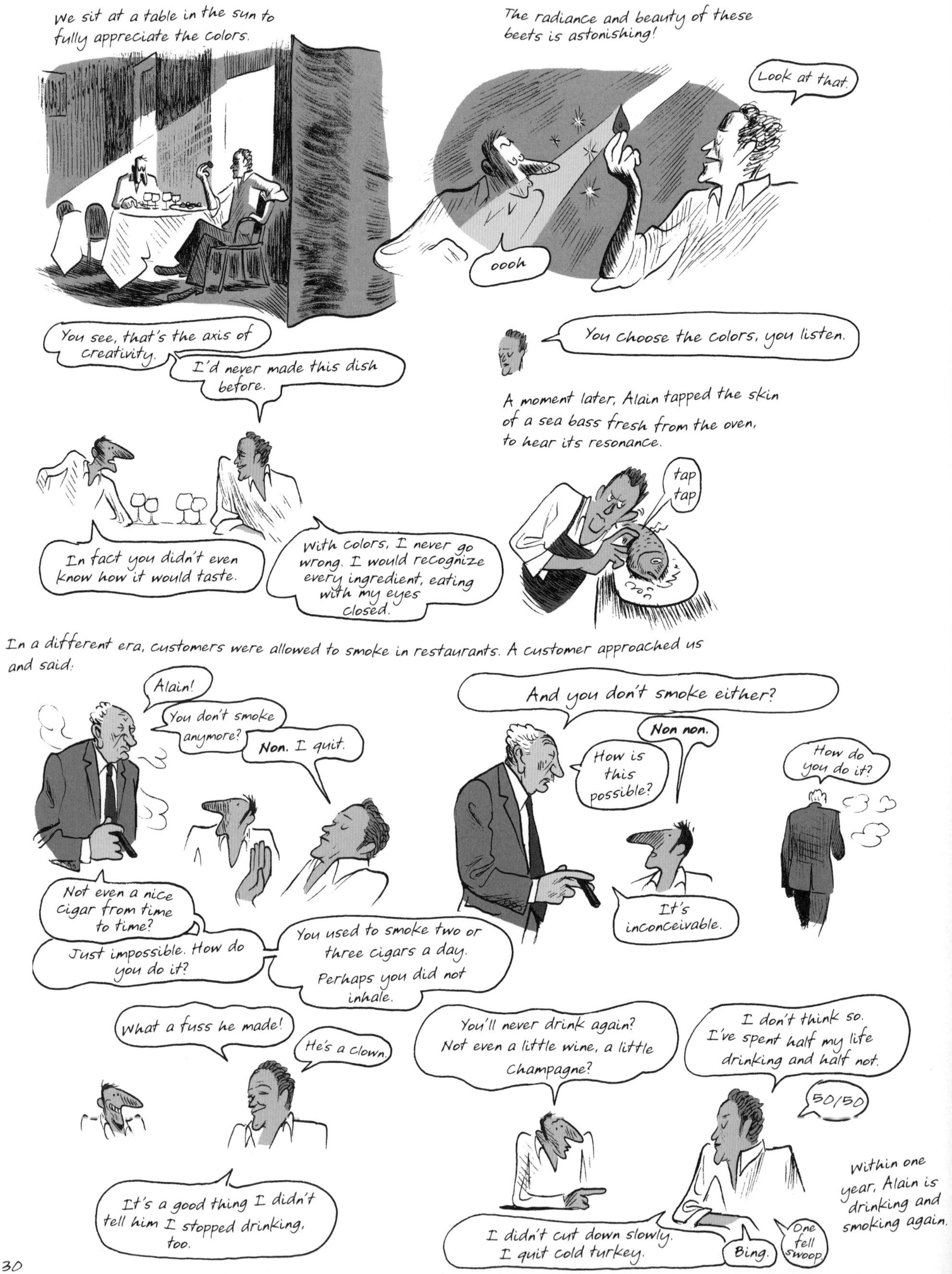
We sit at a table in the sun to fully appreciate the colors.
The radiance and beauty of these beets is astonishing!
Look at that.
oooh
You see, that's the axis of creativity.
I'd never made this dish before.
In fact you didn't even know how it would taste.
With colors, I never go wrong. I would recognize every ingredient, eating with my eyes closed.
You choose the colors, you listen.
A moment later, Alain tapped the skin of a sea bass fresh from the oven, to hear its resonance.
tap tap
In a different era, customers were allowed to smoke in restaurants. A customer approached us and said:
Alain!
You don't smoke anymore?
Non. I quit.
Not even a nice cigar from time to time?
Just impossible. How do you do it?
You used to smoke two or three cigars a day.
Perhaps you did not inhale.
And you don't smoke either?
Non non.
How is this possible?
It's inconceivable.
How do you do it?
What a fuss he made!
He's a clown.
It's a good thing I didn't tell him I stopped drinking, too.
You'll never drink again? Not even a little wine, a little Champagne?
I don't think so. I've spent half my life drinking and half not.
50/50
I didn't cut down slowly. I quit cold turkey.
Bing.
One fell swoop.
Within one year, Alain is drinking and smoking again.

"Pizza-Style" Potato Galettes
with Crudités and Parmesan

∎∎◾◾◦◦∎∎∎

John Dory with Bay Leaves Under the Skin

"Pizza-Style" Potato Galettes with Crudités and Parmesan

SERVES 4

With a spiral slicer, grate 4 large potatoes into fine vermicelli. Place in a hot frying pan with 2 tablespoons of salted butter, and create a galette ½ inch thick. Sprinkle with thyme leaves. On low heat, let it brown for 10 to 12 minutes, making sure to turn it over halfway through. This will be the base of your pizza; it should be crisp on the outside and soft on the inside. When it's done, leave it in the warm pan but remove from the heat. Top your galette with crudités, sliced into thin rounds: 6 young onions, 4 red or yellow beets, and 2 black radishes. Add a "veil" of grated Parmesan, a drizzle of olive oil, and ½ bundle of fresh parsley, chopped. Slide the galette from the pan onto a cutting board, sprinkle with fleur de sel, and cut it into four slices. Serve on warm plates with a spring mix salad and tapenade or a smooth Orléans (or another French) mustard.

Use a 12-inch pan to prepare the galette. Add the toppings sparingly to obtain a good balance between the crispness of the base and the tenderness of the crudités.

To make rounds of crudités, slice them on a Japanese mandoline.

You can also create a summer galette with halved cherry tomatoes, thin rounds of zucchini, and basil leaves.

This galette invites creativity, so allow your imagination free rein in assembling the colors and tastes!

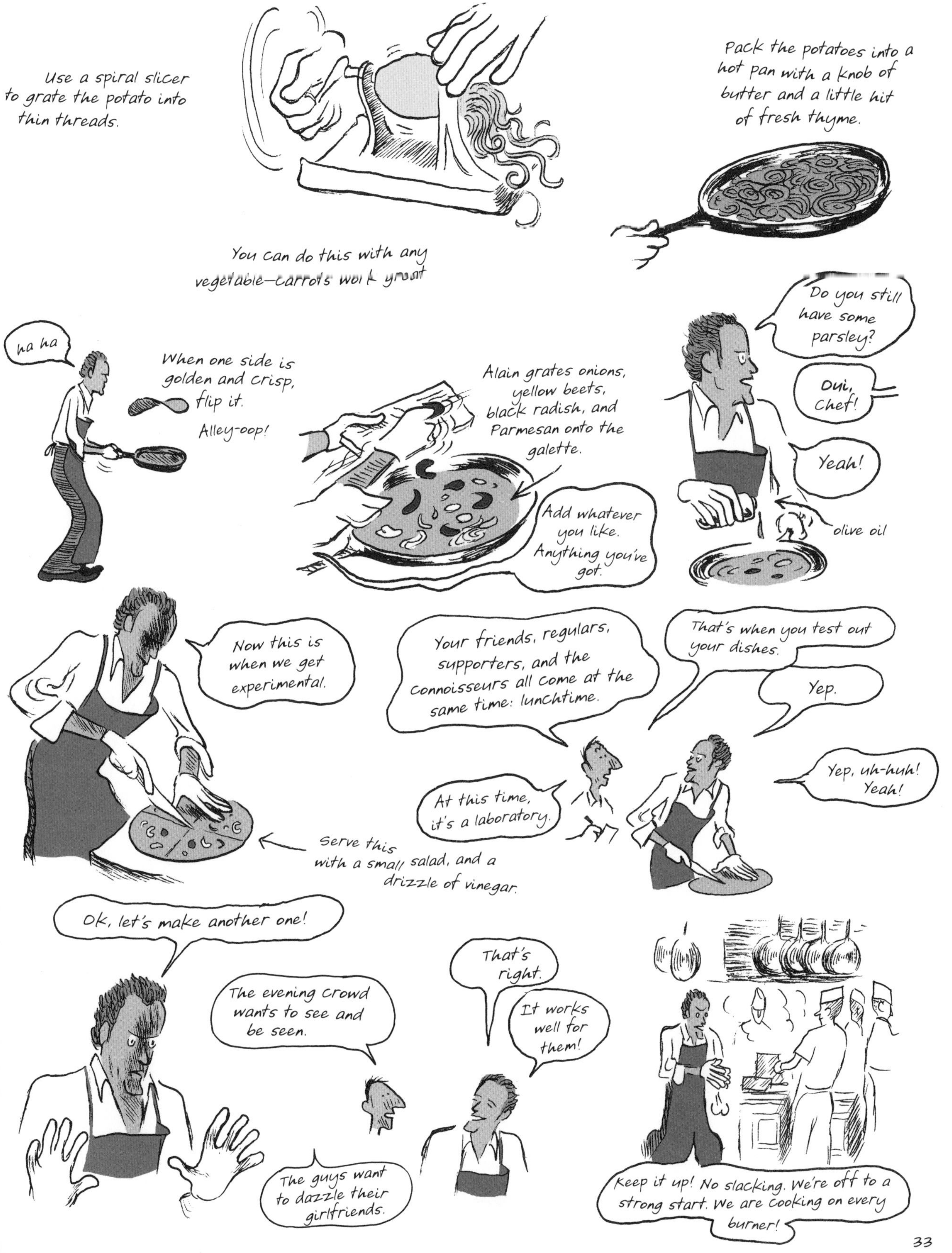

Use a spiral slicer to grate the potato into thin threads.
You can do this with any vegetable—carrots work great
Pack the potatoes into a hot pan with a knob of butter and a little bit of fresh thyme.
ha ha
When one side is golden and crisp, flip it.
Alley-oop!
Alain grates onions, yellow beets, black radish, and Parmesan onto the galette.
Add whatever you like. Anything you've got.
Do you still have some parsley?
Oui, Chef!
Yeah!
olive oil
Now this is when we get experimental.
Your friends, regulars, supporters, and the connoisseurs all come at the same time: lunchtime.
That's when you test out your dishes.
Yep.
Yep, uh-huh! Yeah!
At this time, it's a laboratory.
Serve this with a small salad, and a drizzle of vinegar.
Ok, let's make another one!
The evening crowd wants to see and be seen.
That's right.
It works well for them!
The guys want to dazzle their girlfriends.
Keep it up! No slacking. We're off to a strong start. We are cooking on every burner!

John Dory with Bay Leaves Under the Skin

SERVES 4

With the point of a sharp knife (I use a utility knife), make a slit lengthwise in the skin of a 2¼-pound John Dory or porgy, on each side, without touching the flesh. With both hands, ease the skin away from the flesh, creating a good space between the two, and slide 4 or 5 fresh bay leaves under the skin on each side.

In a large, oval fish frying pan, brown the Dory in a bit of olive oil over high heat, 7 or 8 minutes on each side. Set it on a hot ovenproof serving plate in an oven preheated to 400°F. Allow it to cook for 20 minutes more with the heat turned off and the oven door ajar. Just before serving, pass the John Dory under the broiler, daub it with a chunk of salted butter to give it a good sheen, and show it to your guests. On the still-warm plate, use a fish knife and spatula to remove the fillets. Serve them on warm dishes with a few drops of olive oil, a pinch of fleur de sel, and, above all, the precious juices spooned from the bottom of the cooking plate! Garnish with a seasonal vegetable—young cabbage heart braised in a casserole, or in summer, chopped tomatoes, or eggplant caviar.

Linger over the aroma and taste of the fresh bay leaves; they impart a floral tone and a lovely bitter note to the fish. Increase or reduce the number of bay leaves in the recipe, depending on your taste.

The bay leaves can be replaced by fresh lime leaves, which I prefer. They're harder to come by, though.

You can push hard when you are loosening the skin from the fillets, as the skin is quite sturdy.

A trick for turning the fish over: Stand in front of the sink, place your hand flat over the John Dory, and turn the pan over. This way you won't damage the fish.

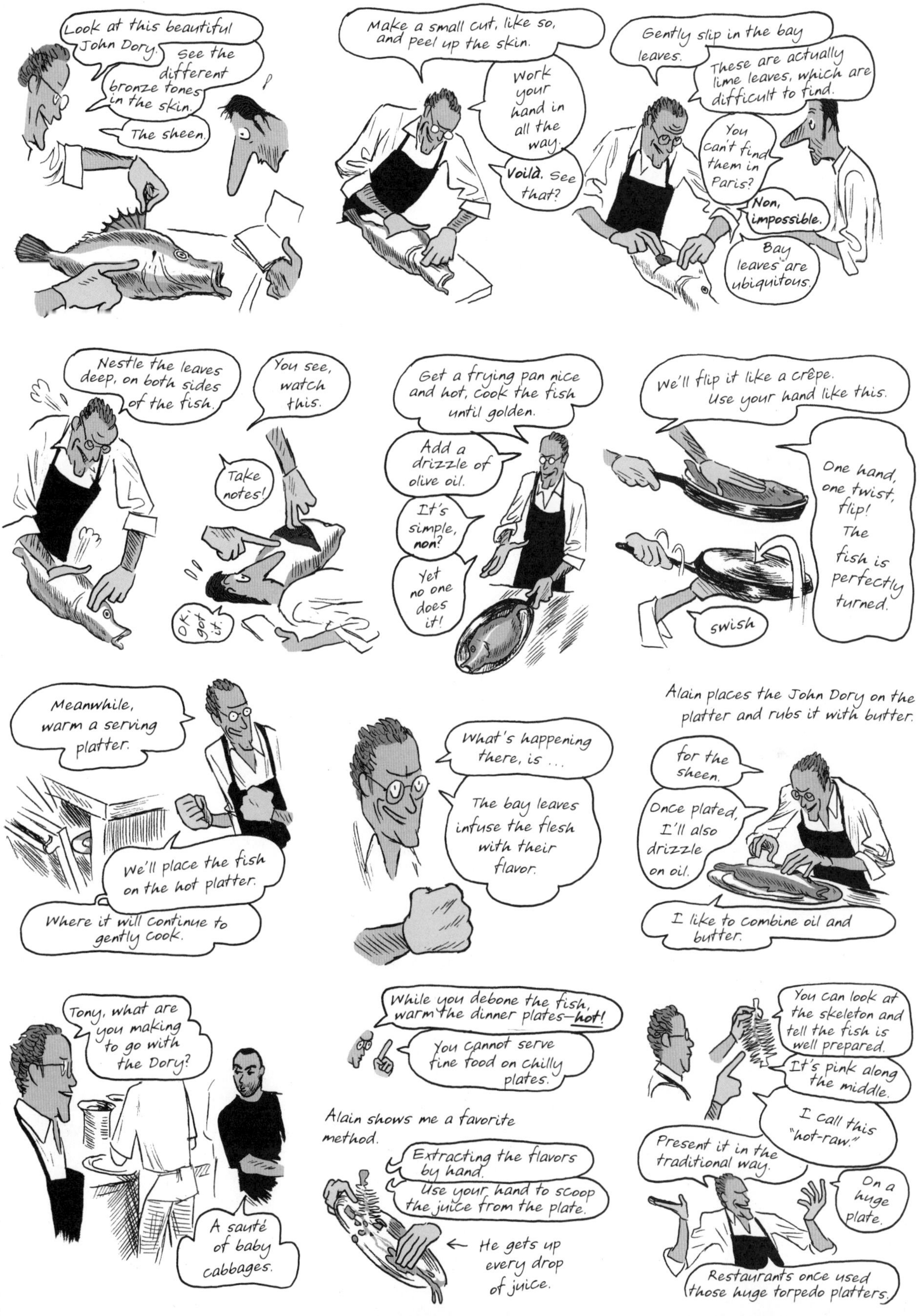
Look at this beautiful John Dory.
See the different bronze tones in the skin.
The sheen.
Make a small cut, like so, and peel up the skin.
Work your hand in all the way.
Voilà. See that?
Gently slip in the bay leaves.
These are actually lime leaves, which are difficult to find.
You can't find them in Paris?
Non, impossible.
Bay leaves are ubiquitous.
Nestle the leaves deep, on both sides of the fish.
You see, watch this.
Take notes!
OK, got it.
Get a frying pan nice and hot, cook the fish until golden.
Add a drizzle of olive oil.
It's simple, non?
Yet no one does it!
We'll flip it like a crêpe. Use your hand like this.
One hand, one twist, flip!
The fish is perfectly turned.
swish
Meanwhile, warm a serving platter.
We'll place the fish on the hot platter.
Where it will continue to gently cook.
What's happening there, is ...
The bay leaves infuse the flesh with their flavor.
Alain places the John Dory on the platter and rubs it with butter.
for the sheen.
Once plated, I'll also drizzle on oil.
I like to combine oil and butter.
Tony, what are you making to go with the Dory?
A sauté of baby cabbages.
While you debone the fish, warm the dinner plates—hot!
You cannot serve fine food on chilly plates.
Alain shows me a favorite method.
Extracting the flavors by hand.
Use your hand to scoop the juice from the plate.
He gets up every drop of juice.
You can look at the skeleton and tell the fish is well prepared.
It's pink along the middle.
I call this "hot-raw."
Present it in the traditional way.
On a huge plate.
Restaurants once used those huge torpedo platters.

PARIS TO TOKYO

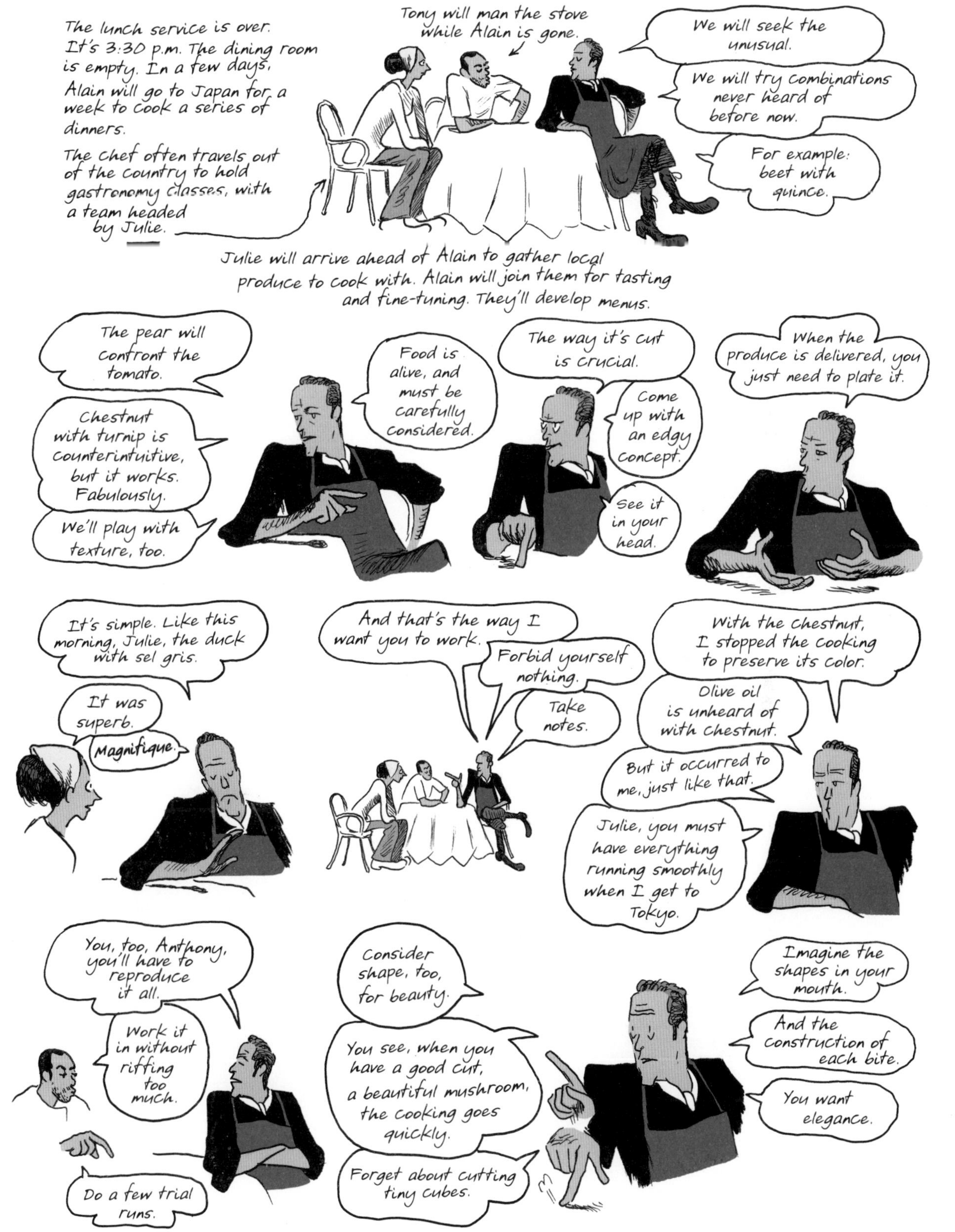
The lunch service is over. It's 3:30 p.m. The dining room is empty. In a few days, Alain will go to Japan for a week to cook a series of dinners.
The chef often travels out of the country to hold gastronomy classes, with a team headed by Julie.
Tony will man the stove while Alain is gone.
We will seek the unusual.
We will try combinations never heard of before now.
For example: beet with quince.
Julie will arrive ahead of Alain to gather local produce to cook with. Alain will join them for tasting and fine-tuning. They'll develop menus.
The pear will confront the tomato.
Chestnut with turnip is counterintuitive, but it works. Fabulously.
We'll play with texture, too.
Food is alive, and must be carefully considered.
The way it's cut is crucial.
Come up with an edgy concept.
See it in your head.
When the produce is delivered, you just need to plate it.
It's simple. Like this morning, Julie, the duck with sel gris.
It was superb.
Magnifique.
And that's the way I want you to work.
Forbid yourself nothing.
Take notes.
With the chestnut, I stopped the cooking to preserve its color.
Olive oil is unheard of with chestnut.
But it occurred to me, just like that.
Julie, you must have everything running smoothly when I get to Tokyo.
You, too, Anthony, you'll have to reproduce it all.
Work it in without riffing too much.
Do a few trial runs.
Consider shape, too, for beauty.
You see, when you have a good cut, a beautiful mushroom, the cooking goes quickly.
Forget about cutting tiny cubes.
Imagine the shapes in your mouth.
And the construction of each bite.
You want elegance.

THE HARE

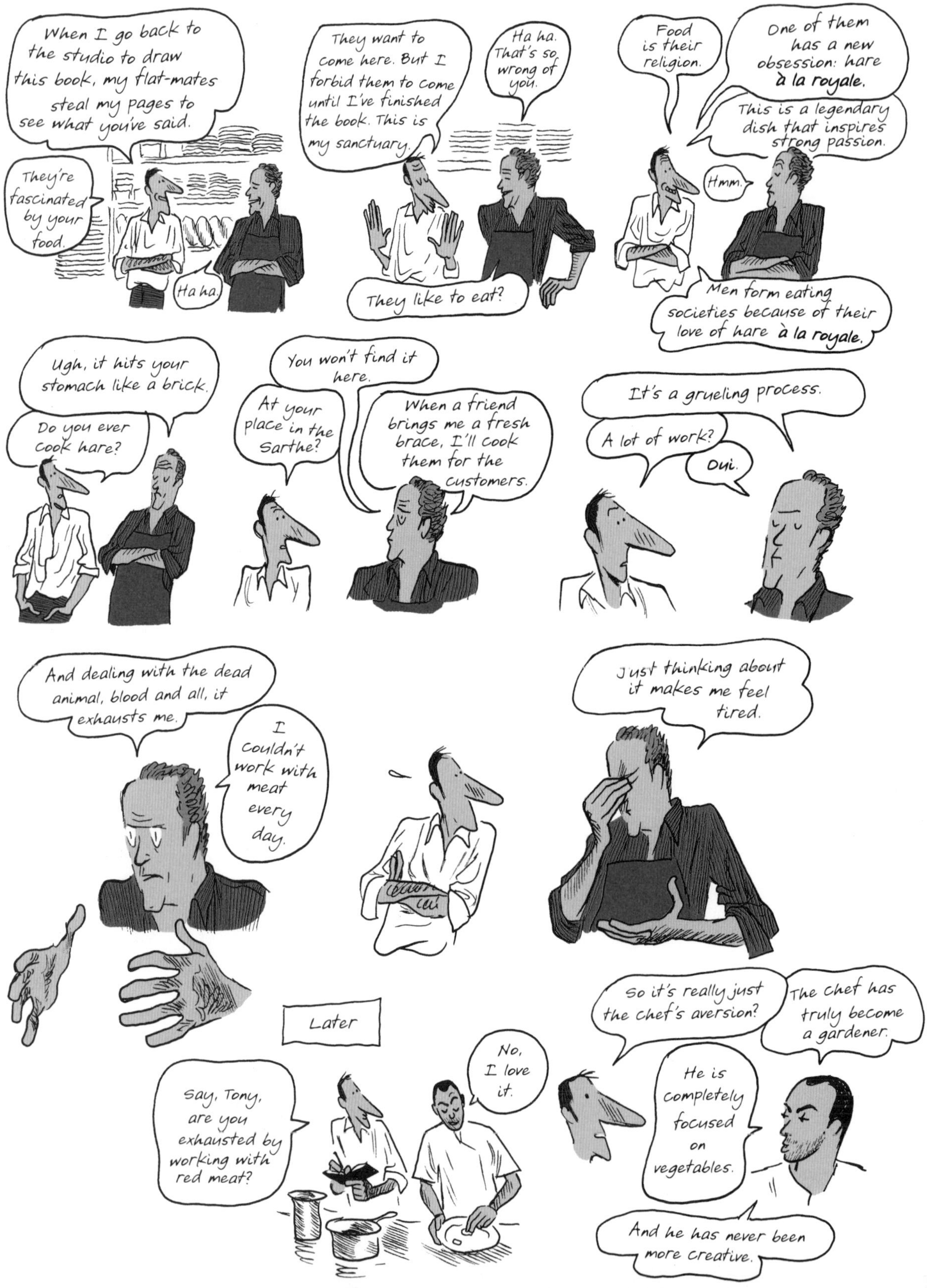

When I go back to the studio to draw this book, my flat-mates steal my pages to see what you've said.
They're fascinated by your food.
Ha ha.
They want to come here. But I forbid them to come until I've finished the book. This is my sanctuary.
Ha ha. That's so wrong of you.
They like to eat?
Food is their religion.
One of them has a new obsession: hare **à la royale.**
This is a legendary dish that inspires strong passion.
Hmm.
Men form eating societies because of their love of hare **à la royale.**
Do you ever cook hare?
Ugh, it hits your stomach like a brick.
At your place in the Sarthe?
You won't find it here.
When a friend brings me a fresh brace, I'll cook them for the customers.
A lot of work?
It's a grueling process.
Oui.
And dealing with the dead animal, blood and all, it exhausts me.
I couldn't work with meat every day.
Just thinking about it makes me feel tired.
Later
Say, Tony, are you exhausted by working with red meat?
No, I love it.
So it's really just the chef's aversion?
The chef has truly become a gardener.
He is completely focused on vegetables.
And he has never been more creative.

Hot-Cold Eggs with Maple Syrup

∎∎∎◢∎∎∎∎

Purple Passion with Acacia Honey

Hot-Cold Eggs with Maple Syrup

SERVES 4

With an egg topper (sort of an eggshell punch), delicately score 8 eggs, leaving a clean line around each shell. Then, with the corner of a razor blade, go a little deeper, following the demarcated line taking the top off. Finally, with a gentle, deft motion, pour off the egg white, keeping the yolk in the palm of your hand. Without breaking it, return the yolk to its shell. Put the eggs in an egg carton, cover with plastic wrap, and store in the refrigerator. Now, in a chilled bowl, whip 1 cup of heavy cream (chilled in the freezer) with a few grains of fleur de sel, a generous pinch of quatre épices, and 1 tablespoon of sherry vinegar. Whip the cream until it coats the back of a spoon, and adjust the spices and vinegar to your taste. Chill in a pastry bag.

Heat a pan of water over low heat to 160°F (you can quickly dip your finger in without burning yourself!). Place the eggshells on the surface of the steaming water—they will float like tiny ships!* Allow 3 to 4 minutes of cooking time; the yolk should be warm but still runny, like a soft-boiled egg. Watch the edge of the yolk: a white line will form. Place each shell in an egg cup, and sprinkle with 1 teaspoon of chopped chives. Cover with a nice dollop of whipped cream from the pastry bag, and drizzle with maple syrup. Serve immediately, without stirring, but stick a demitasse spoon all the way into the shell to reveal the warmth of the egg and the chill of the cream.

Quatre épices, *for those who aren't familiar with it, consists of ginger, white pepper, nutmeg, and cloves. It's found in all good spice shops.*

* *The weight of the yolk will stabilize the eggshell in the water.*

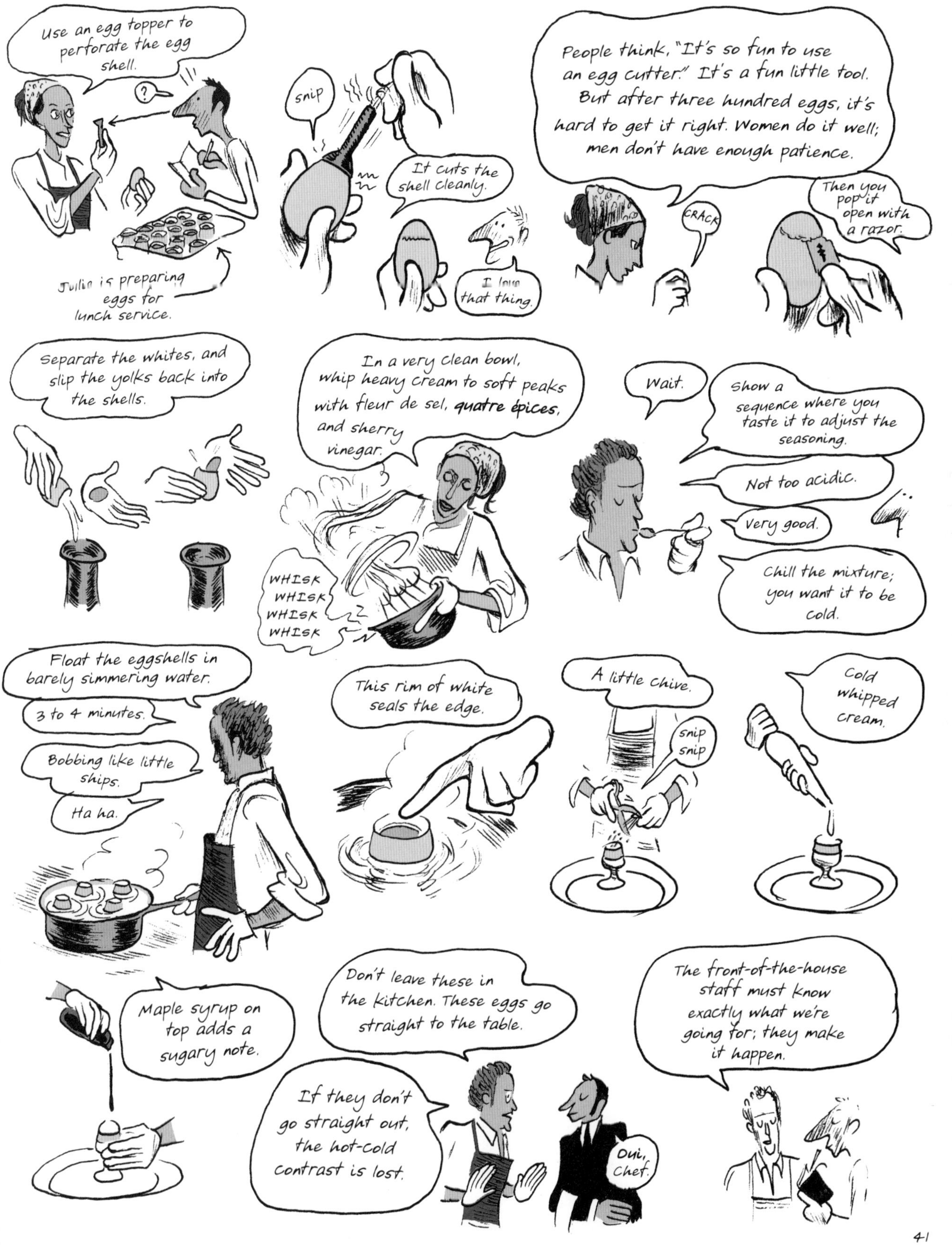
Use an egg topper to perforate the egg shell.
?
Julia is preparing eggs for lunch service.
snip
It cuts the shell cleanly.
I love that thing.
People think, "It's so fun to use an egg cutter." It's a fun little tool. But after three hundred eggs, it's hard to get it right. Women do it well; men don't have enough patience.
CRACK
Then you pop it open with a razor.
Separate the whites, and slip the yolks back into the shells.
In a very clean bowl, whip heavy cream to soft peaks with fleur de sel, **quatre épices**, and sherry vinegar.
WHISK
WHISK
WHISK
WHISK
Wait.
Show a sequence where you taste it to adjust the seasoning.
Not too acidic.
Very good.
Chill the mixture; you want it to be cold.
Float the eggshells in barely simmering water.
3 to 4 minutes.
Bobbing like little ships.
Ha ha.
This rim of white seals the edge.
A little chive.
snip snip
Cold whipped cream.
Maple syrup on top adds a sugary note.
Don't leave these in the kitchen. These eggs go straight to the table.
If they don't go straight out, the hot-cold contrast is lost.
Oui, Chef.
The front-of-the-house staff must know exactly what we're going for; they make it happen.

Purple Passion with Acacia Honey

SERVES 4

On a plate, create a pretty bouquet in shades of purple: a beautiful red beet cooked in its skin, the leaves of ½ bunch of purple basil, 1 bunch of muscat grapes, and ½ small poivron doux chocolat (chocolate sweet pepper). This pepper, a variety whose color evokes the reddish-brown hues of cocoa powder, has a very elegant bitter taste.

In a large sauté pan over low heat, melt 2 tablespoons of salted butter along with 1 tablespoon of acacia honey. Let the butter foam for a few seconds, and then add, without piling them up, the beet, cut into ¼-inch-thick rounds; the grapes; ½ chocolate sweet pepper, grated; and the purple basil leaves. Cook for 15 to 20 minutes. The liquid from the grapes will seep into the butter and honey, forming a lovely purple sauce at the bottom of the pan. On warmed plates, keep the purple fruit-and-vegetable compote separate from the sauce. Serve right away with vanilla or rosemary ice cream.

For the beets, choose the Crapaudine variety (a French heirloom variety), if you can, and cook it in its skin in salted water. Do not overcook, and allow it to cool in the cooking water. You can add the beet tops to the sauté pan for the compote.

If your basil is flowering, add the flowers to the compote.

For rosemary or sage ice cream, use a recipe for vanilla ice cream, and replace the vanilla beans with one of the aromatic herbs.

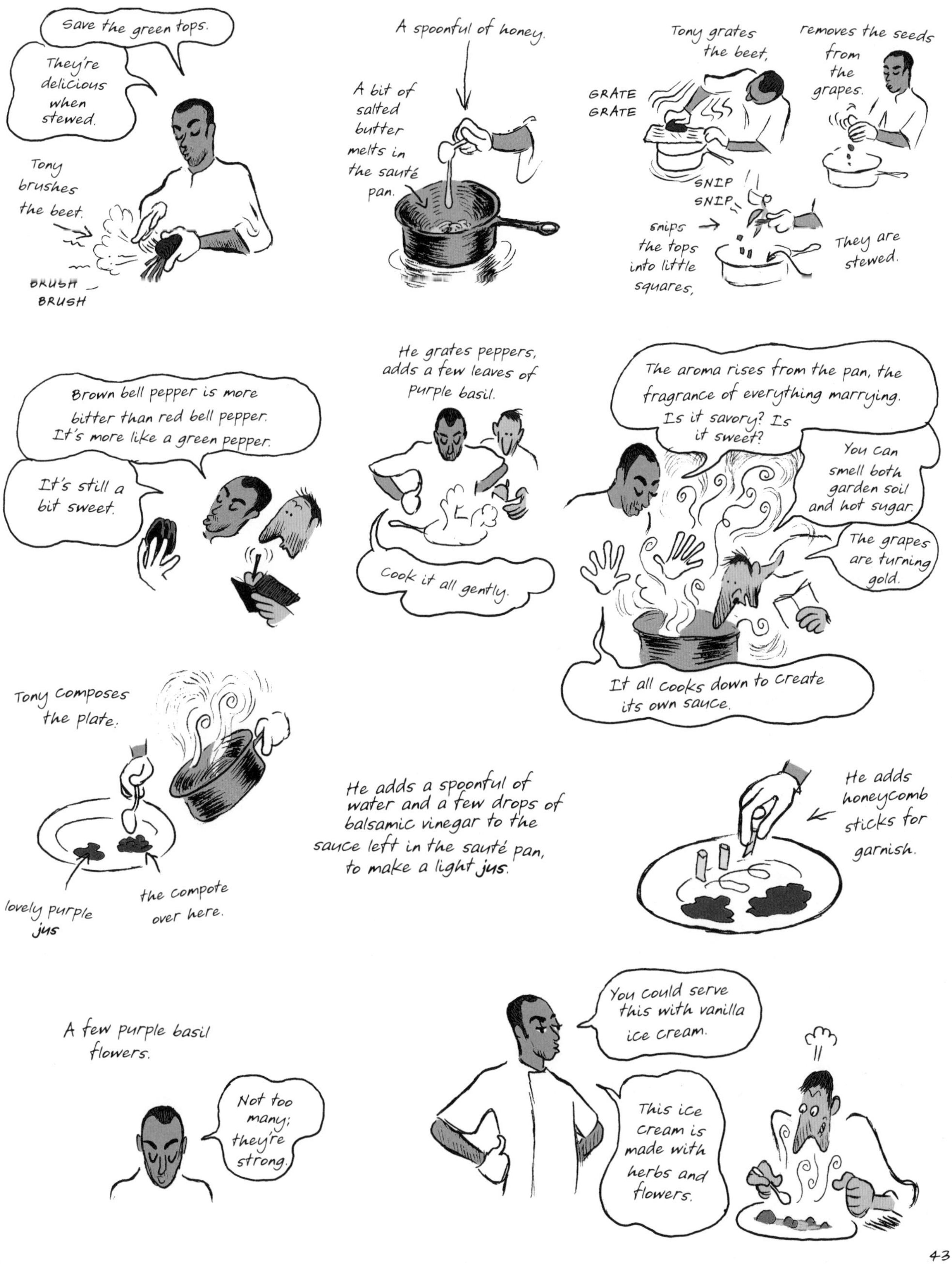
Save the green tops.
They're delicious when stewed.
Tony brushes the beet.
BRUSH BRUSH
A spoonful of honey.
A bit of salted butter melts in the sauté pan.
Tony grates the beet,
GRATE GRATE
removes the seeds from the grapes.
SNIP SNIP
snips the tops into little squares,
They are stewed.
Brown bell pepper is more bitter than red bell pepper. It's more like a green pepper.
It's still a bit sweet.
He grates peppers, adds a few leaves of purple basil.
Cook it all gently.
The aroma rises from the pan, the fragrance of everything marrying. Is it savory? Is it sweet?
You can smell both garden soil and hot sugar.
The grapes are turning gold.
It all cooks down to create its own sauce.
Tony composes the plate.
lovely purple jus
the compote over here.
He adds a spoonful of water and a few drops of balsamic vinegar to the sauce left in the sauté pan, to make a light jus.
He adds honeycomb sticks for garnish.
A few purple basil flowers.
Not too many; they're strong.
You could serve this with vanilla ice cream.
This ice cream is made with herbs and flowers.

JULIE

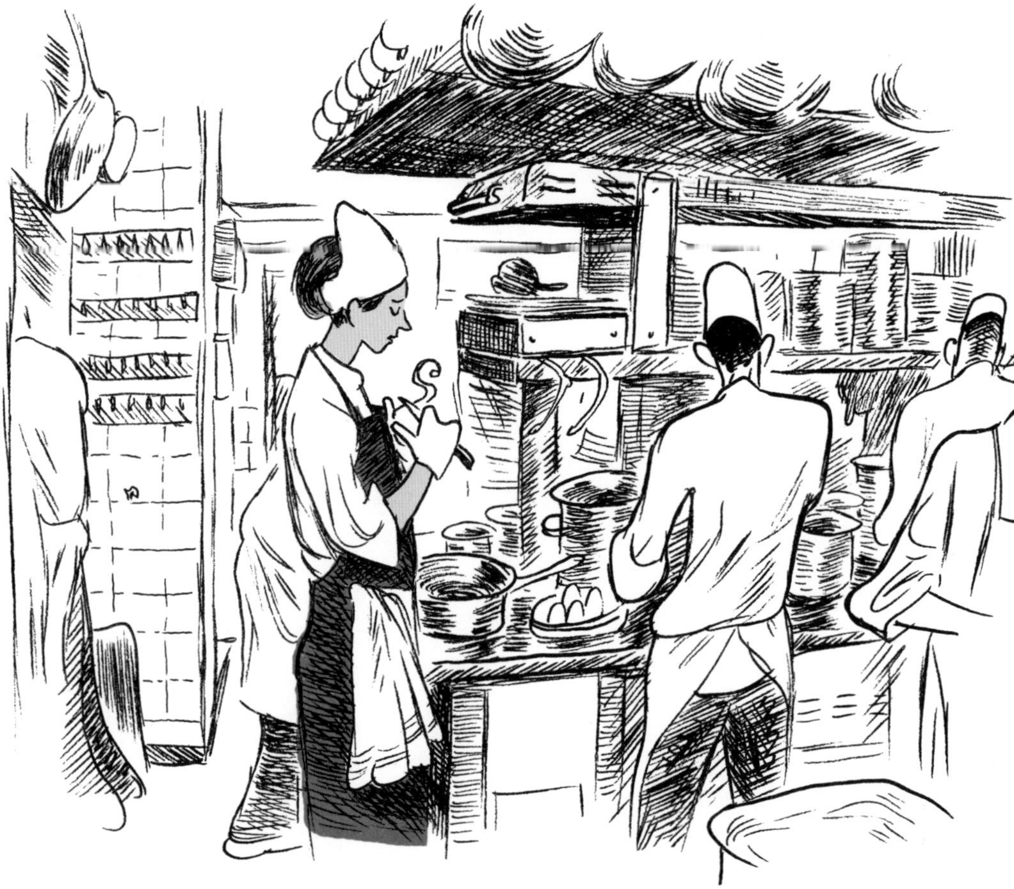

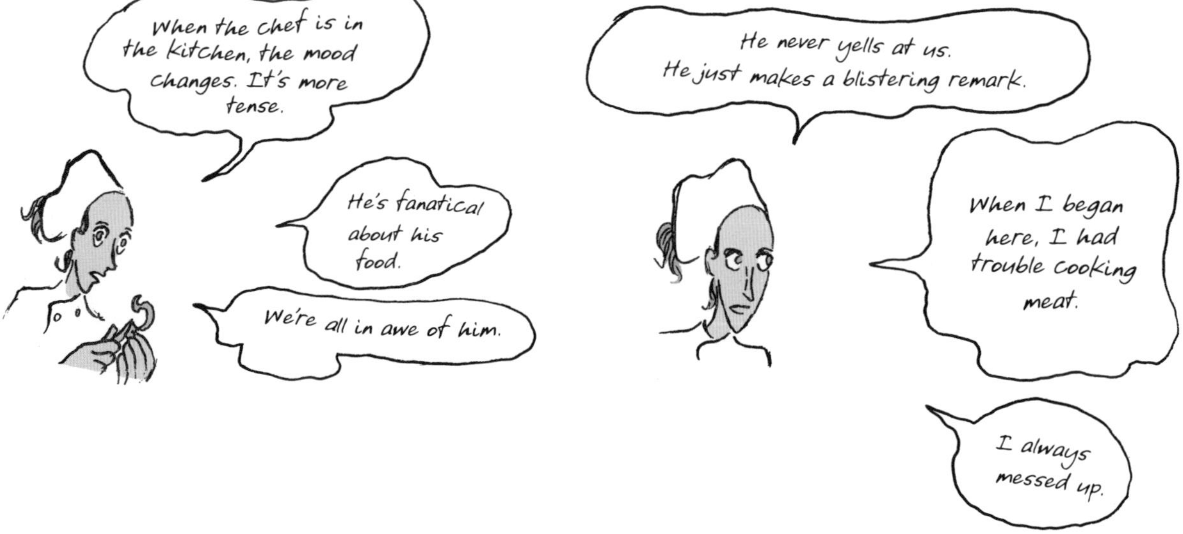

When the chef is in the kitchen, the mood changes. It's more tense.
He's fanatical about his food.
We're all in awe of him.
He never yells at us. He just makes a blistering remark.
When I began here, I had trouble cooking meat.
I always messed up.

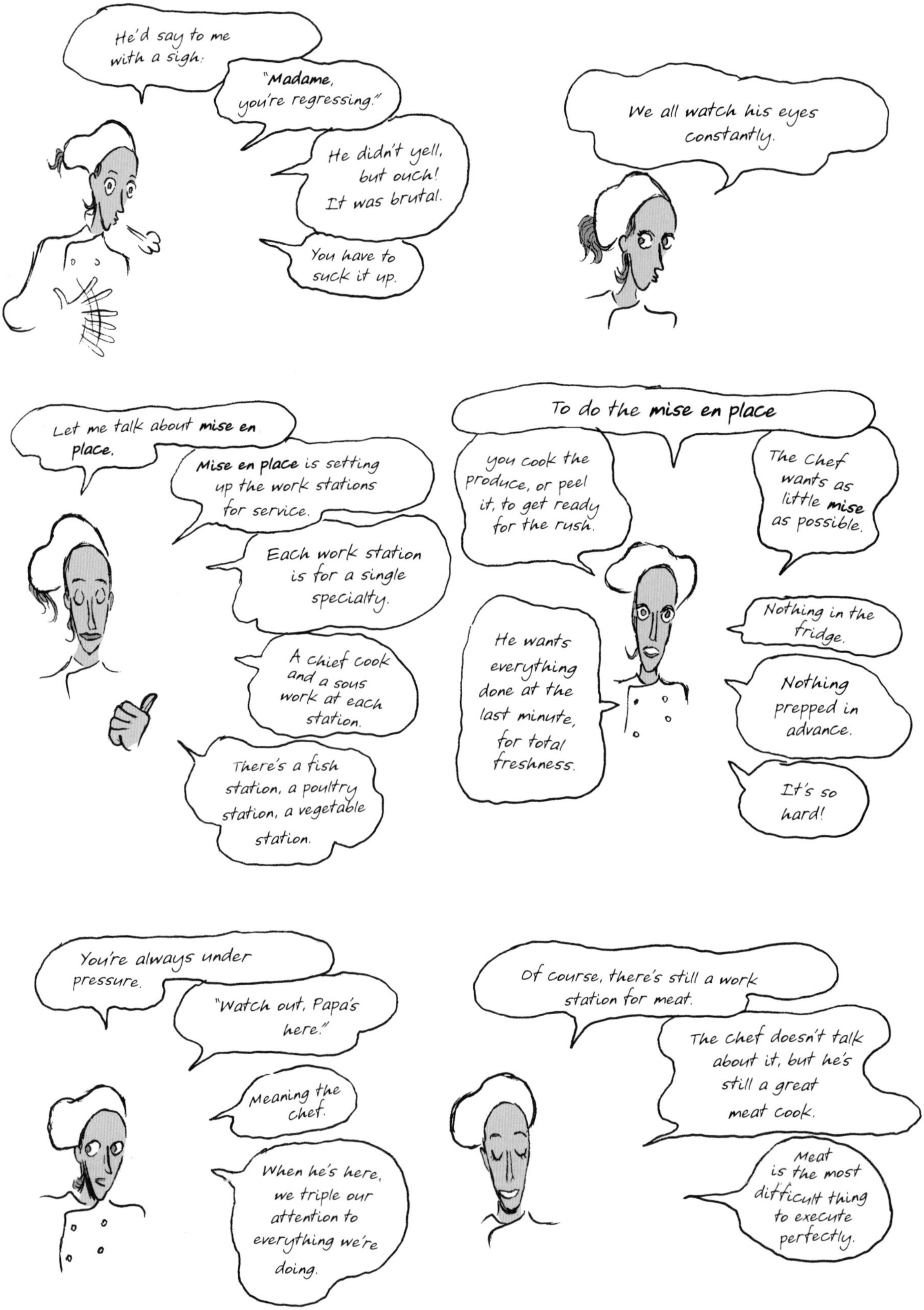
He'd say to me with a sigh:
"**Madame**, you're regressing."
He didn't yell, but ouch! It was brutal.
You have to suck it up.
We all watch his eyes constantly.
Let me talk about **mise en place**.
Mise en place is setting up the work stations for service.
Each work station is for a single specialty.
A chief cook and a sous work at each station.
There's a fish station, a poultry station, a vegetable station.
To do the **mise en place**
you cook the produce, or peel it, to get ready for the rush.
The Chef wants as little **mise** as possible.
He wants everything done at the last minute, for total freshness.
Nothing in the fridge.
Nothing prepped in advance.
It's so hard!
You're always under pressure.
"Watch out, Papa's here."
Meaning the chef.
When he's here, we triple our attention to everything we're doing.
Of course, there's still a work station for meat.
The chef doesn't talk about it, but he's still a great meat cook.
Meat is the most difficult thing to execute perfectly.

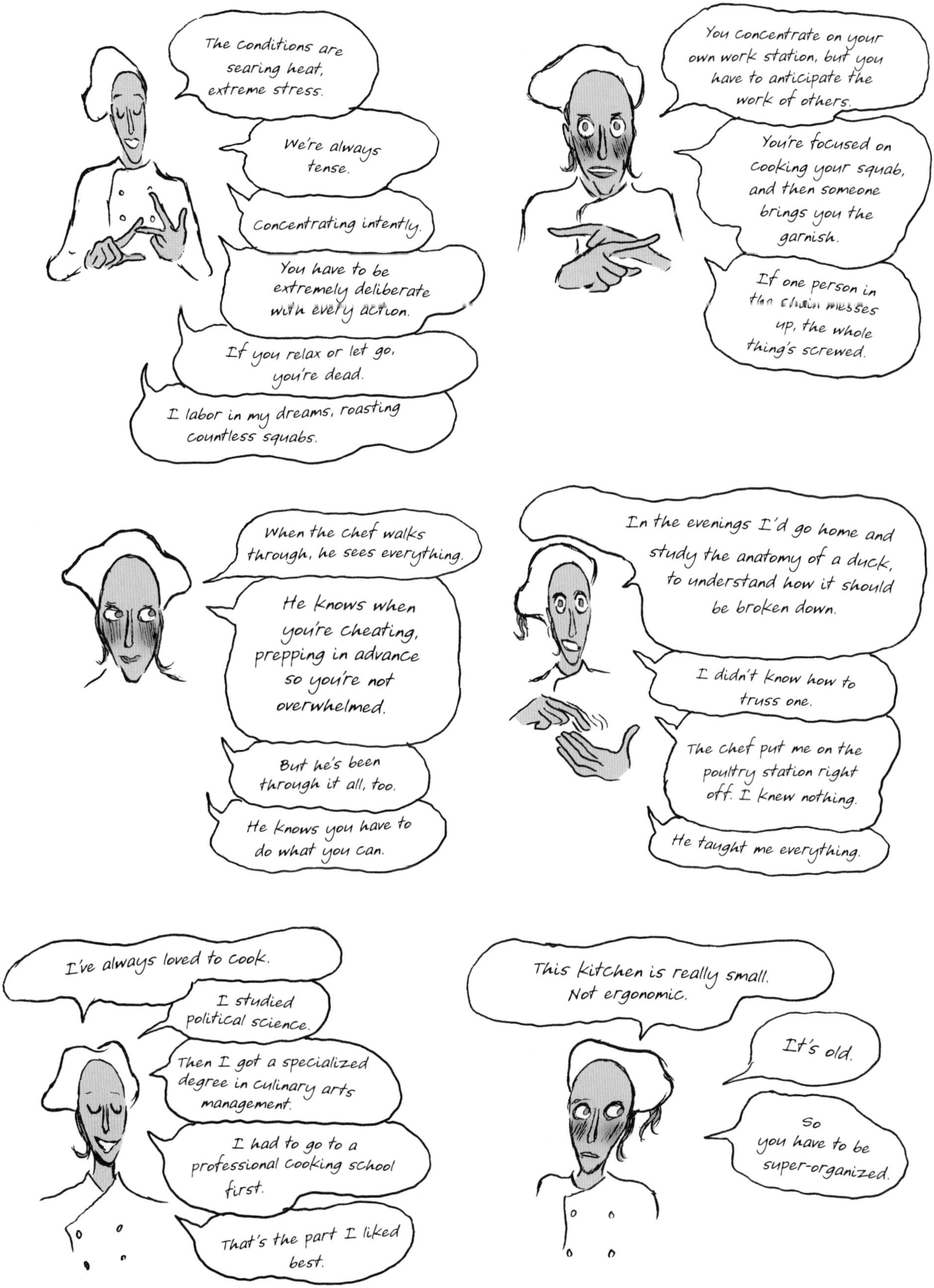

The conditions are searing heat, extreme stress.
We're always tense.
Concentrating intently.
You have to be extremely deliberate with every action.
If you relax or let go, you're dead.
I labor in my dreams, roasting countless squabs.
You concentrate on your own work station, but you have to anticipate the work of others.
You're focused on cooking your squab, and then someone brings you the garnish.
If one person in the chain messes up, the whole thing's screwed.
When the chef walks through, he sees everything.
He knows when you're cheating, prepping in advance so you're not overwhelmed.
But he's been through it all, too.
He knows you have to do what you can.
In the evenings I'd go home and study the anatomy of a duck, to understand how it should be broken down.
I didn't know how to truss one.
The chef put me on the poultry station right off. I knew nothing.
He taught me everything.
I've always loved to cook.
I studied political science.
Then I got a specialized degree in culinary arts management.
I had to go to a professional cooking school first.
That's the part I liked best.
This kitchen is really small. Not ergonomic.
It's old.
So you have to be super-organized.

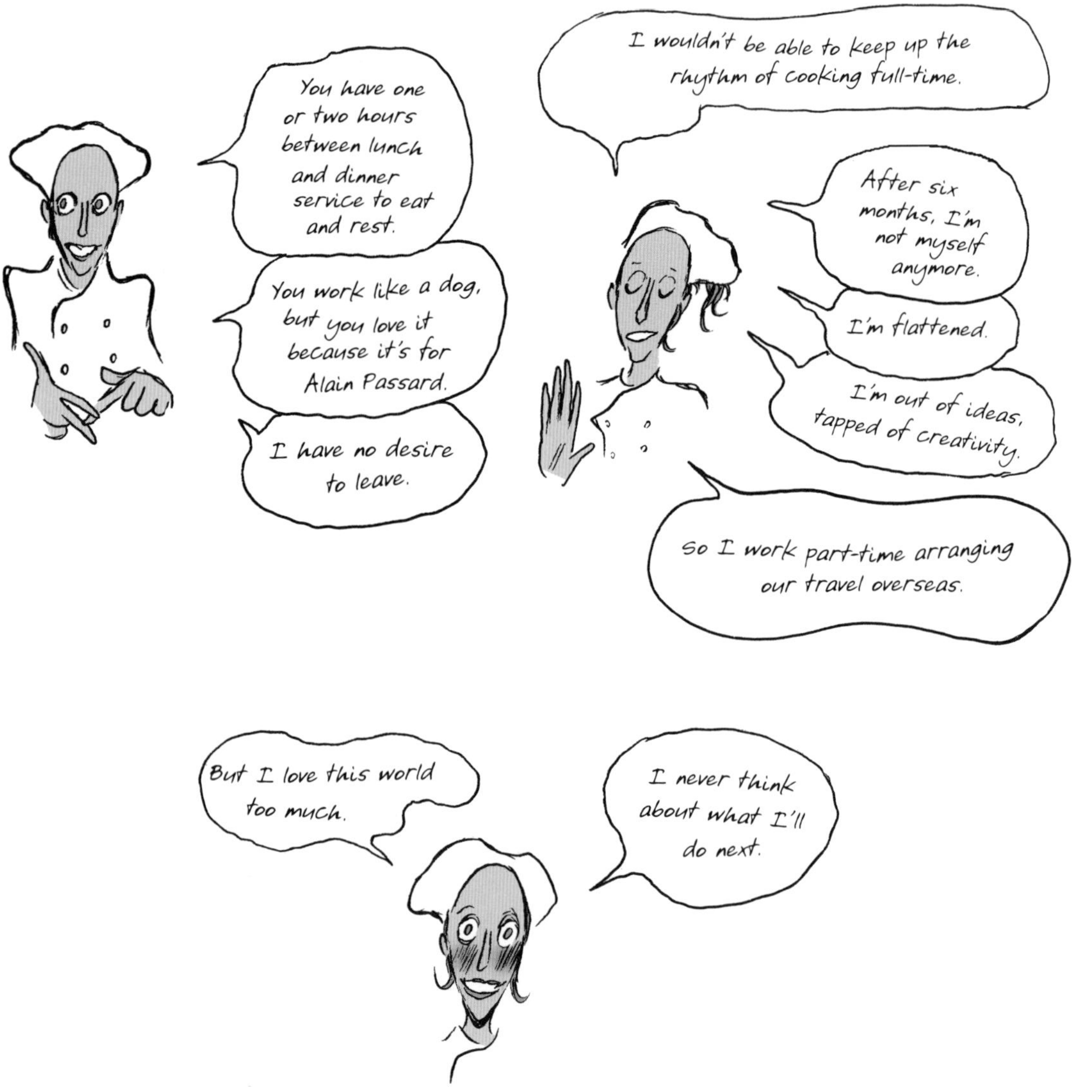
You have one or two hours between lunch and dinner service to eat and rest.
You work like a dog, but you love it because it's for Alain Passard.
I have no desire to leave.
I wouldn't be able to keep up the rhythm of cooking full-time.
After six months, I'm not myself anymore.
I'm flattened.
I'm out of ideas, tapped of creativity.
So I work part-time arranging our travel overseas.
But I love this world too much.
I never think about what I'll do next.

Potato Paillasse with Sage and Young Garlic

Potato Paillasse* with Sage and Young Garlic

SERVES 4

In a large bowl, grate 10 peeled medium, raw potatoes; opt for a very starchy variety (like russet) so your **paillasse** will hold together well as it cooks. To the grated potatoes, add the peeled, crushed cloves of 2 small heads of garlic and the deveined leaves of 4 sprigs of sage. In a hot frying pan with 2 tablespoons of salted butter, make the **paillasse** by spreading out the grated potato, garlic, and sage mixture with a spoon. Allow it to cook on low heat for 10 minutes on each side, until golden. Cut it into quarters and serve, sprinkled with fleur de sel, and topped with a nubbin of sweet butter.

*The **paillasse** should be cooked in a large frying pan 10 inches in diameter.*

*Your **paillasse** should be no thicker than ½ inch, so it's nice and crisp on the outside and tender on the inside.*

To devein a sage leaf, fold the leaf in half lengthwise and pull out the central vein with your fingers.

The garlic and sage should be balanced; be sure to taste and correct.

A salad of spring greens tossed with hazelnut oil and sherry vinegar makes a perfect accompaniment to this dish.

*A rustic pancake of straw-cut potatoes

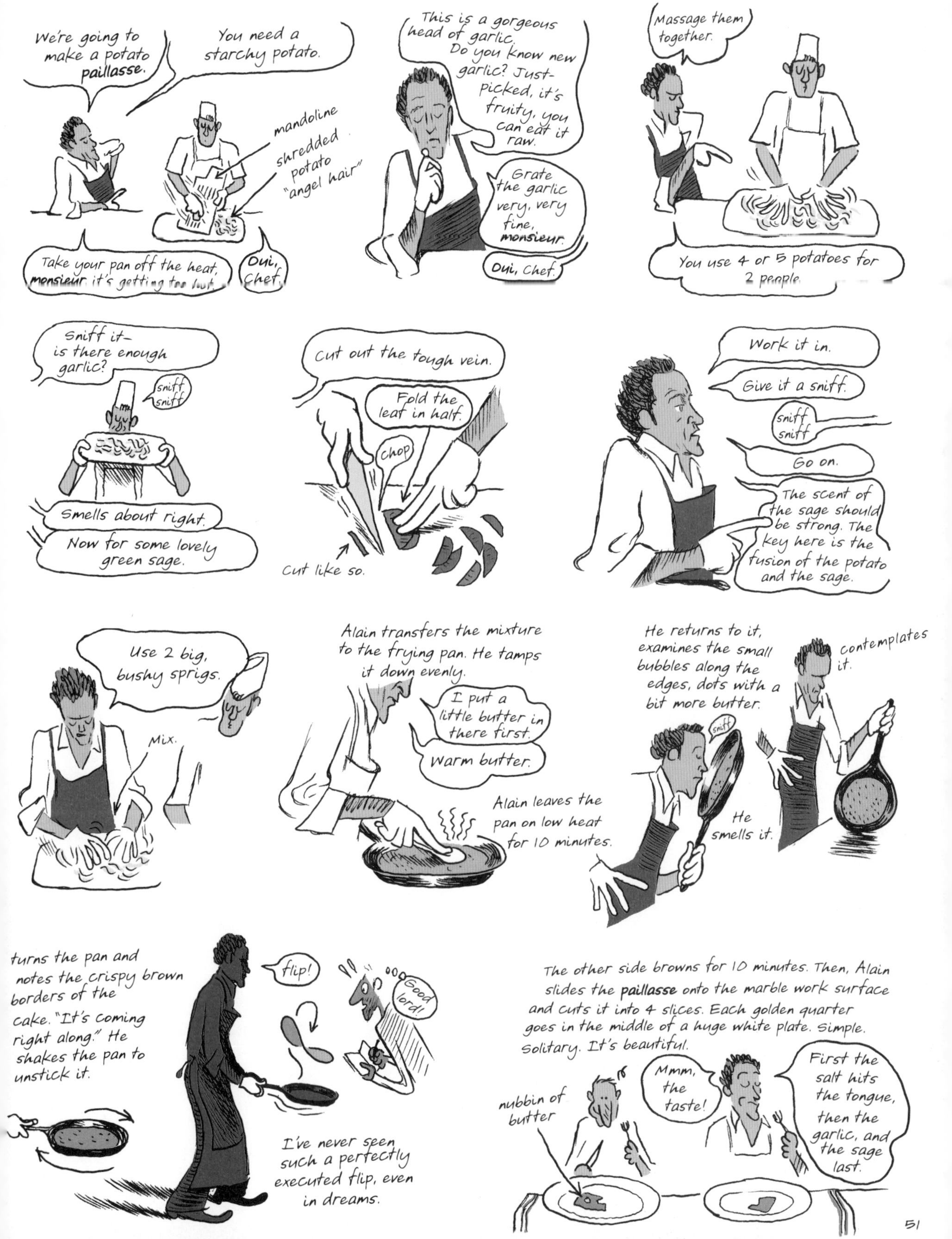

We're going to make a potato paillasse.
You need a starchy potato.
mandoline
shredded potato "angel hair"
Take your pan off the heat, monsieur, it's getting too hot.
Oui, Chef.
This is a gorgeous head of garlic. Do you know new garlic? Just-picked, it's fruity, you can eat it raw.
Grate the garlic very, very fine, monsieur.
Oui, Chef.
Massage them together.
You use 4 or 5 potatoes for 2 people.
Sniff it— is there enough garlic?
sniff, sniff
Smells about right.
Now for some lovely green sage.
Cut out the tough vein.
Fold the leaf in half.
chop
Cut like so.
Work it in.
Give it a sniff.
sniff sniff
Go on.
The scent of the sage should be strong. The key here is the fusion of the potato and the sage.
Use 2 big, bushy sprigs.
Mix.
Alain transfers the mixture to the frying pan. He tamps it down evenly.
I put a little butter in there first.
Warm butter.
Alain leaves the pan on low heat for 10 minutes.
He returns to it, examines the small bubbles along the edges, dots with a bit more butter.
sniff
He smells it.
contemplates it.
turns the pan and notes the crispy brown borders of the cake. "It's coming right along." He shakes the pan to unstick it.
flip!
Good lord!
I've never seen such a perfectly executed flip, even in dreams.
The other side browns for 10 minutes. Then, Alain slides the paillasse onto the marble work surface and cuts it into 4 slices. Each golden quarter goes in the middle of a huge white plate. Simple. Solitary. It's beautiful.
nubbin of butter
Mmm, the taste!
First the salt hits the tongue, then the garlic, and the sage last.

BOUQUET OF ROSES

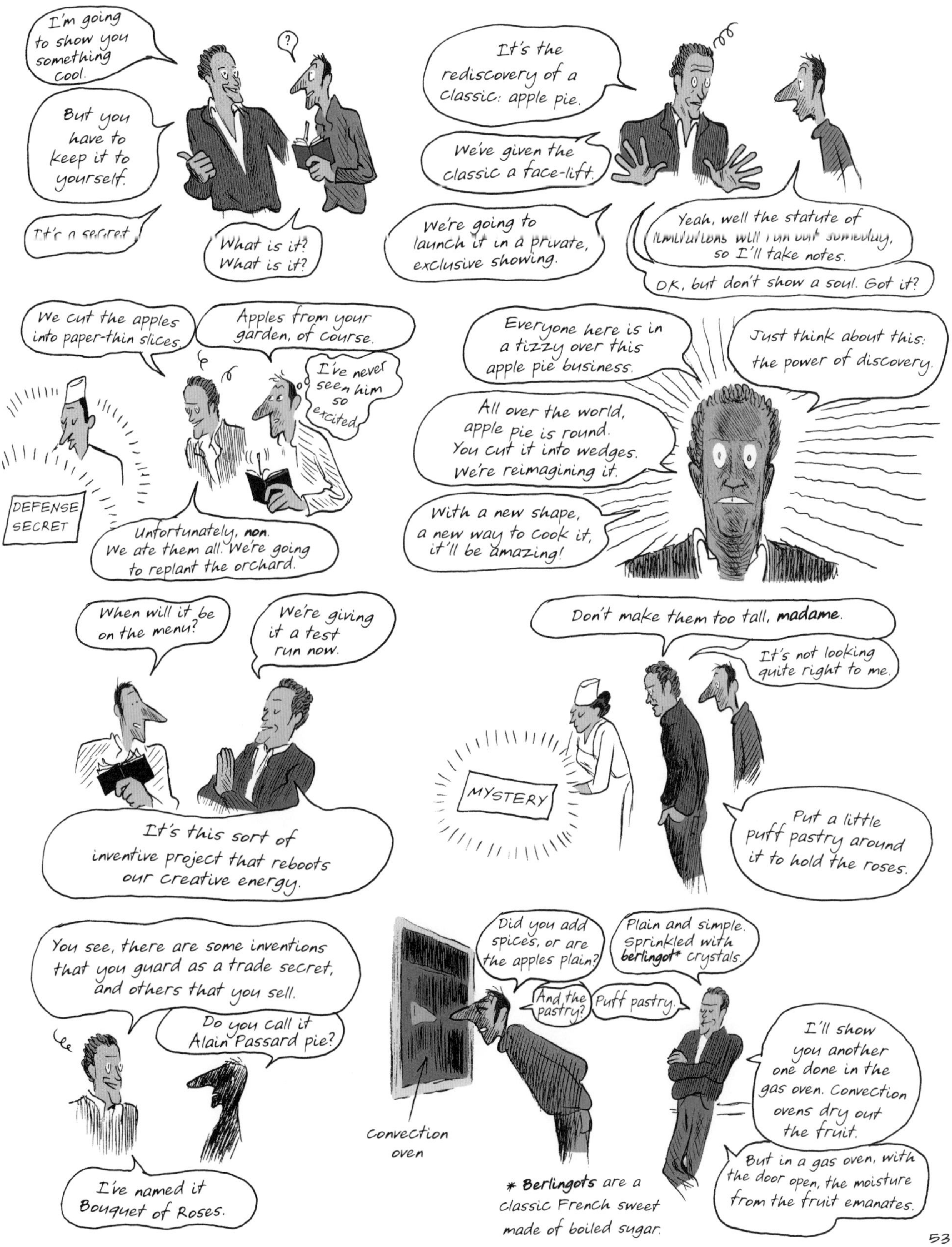

I'm going to show you something cool.
But you have to keep it to yourself.
It's a secret.
?
What is it? What is it?
It's the rediscovery of a classic: apple pie.
We've given the classic a face-lift.
We're going to launch it in a private, exclusive showing.
Yeah, well the statute of limitations will run out someday, so I'll take notes.
OK, but don't show a soul. Got it?
We cut the apples into paper-thin slices.
Apples from your garden, of course.
I've never seen him so excited.
DEFENSE SECRET
Unfortunately, **non**. We ate them all. We're going to replant the orchard.
Everyone here is in a tizzy over this apple pie business.
Just think about this: the power of discovery.
All over the world, apple pie is round. You cut it into wedges. We're reimagining it.
With a new shape, a new way to cook it, it'll be amazing!
When will it be on the menu?
We're giving it a test run now.
It's this sort of inventive project that reboots our creative energy.
Don't make them too tall, **madame**.
It's not looking quite right to me.
MYSTERY
Put a little puff pastry around it to hold the roses.
You see, there are some inventions that you guard as a trade secret, and others that you sell.
Do you call it Alain Passard pie?
I've named it Bouquet of Roses.
Did you add spices, or are the apples plain?
Plain and simple. Sprinkled with **berlingot*** crystals.
And the pastry?
Puff pastry.
I'll show you another one done in the gas oven. Convection ovens dry out the fruit.
But in a gas oven, with the door open, the moisture from the fruit emanates.
Convection oven

* **Berlingots** are a classic French sweet made of boiled sugar.

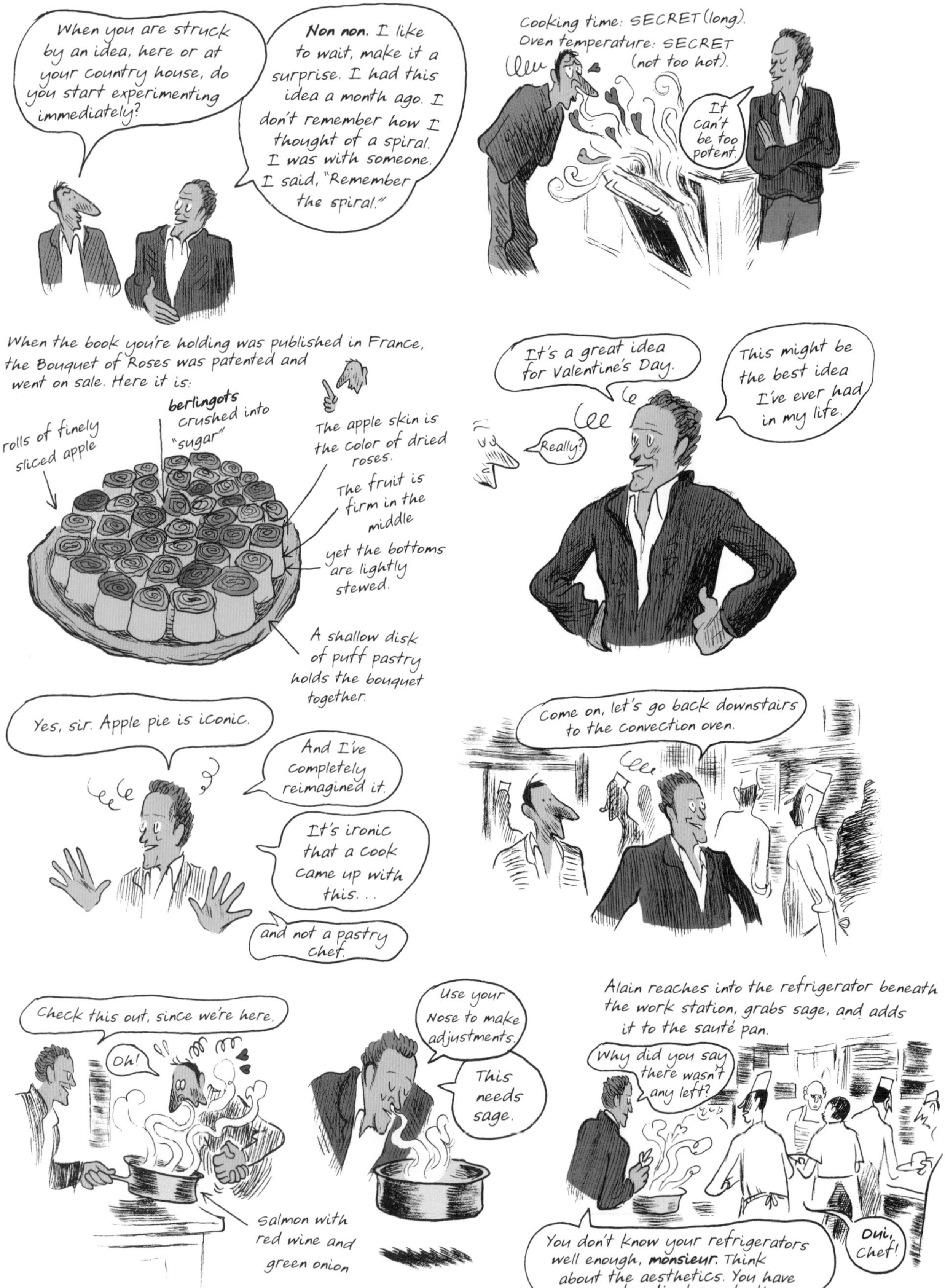
When you are struck by an idea, here or at your country house, do you start experimenting immediately?
Non non. I like to wait, make it a surprise. I had this idea a month ago. I don't remember how I thought of a spiral. I was with someone. I said, "Remember the spiral."
Cooking time: SECRET (long). Oven temperature: SECRET (not too hot).
It can't be too potent.
When the book you're holding was published in France, the Bouquet of Roses was patented and went on sale. Here it is:
rolls of finely sliced apple
berlingots crushed into "sugar"
The apple skin is the color of dried roses.
The fruit is firm in the middle
yet the bottoms are lightly stewed.
A shallow disk of puff pastry holds the bouquet together.
It's a great idea for Valentine's Day.
Really?
This might be the best idea I've ever had in my life.
Yes, sir. Apple pie is iconic.
And I've completely reimagined it.
It's ironic that a cook came up with this. . .
and not a pastry chef.
Come on, let's go back downstairs to the convection oven.
Check this out, since we're here.
Oh!
Salmon with red wine and green onion
Use your Nose to make adjustments.
This needs sage.
Alain reaches into the refrigerator beneath the work station, grabs sage, and adds it to the sauté pan.
Why did you say there wasn't any left?
You don't know your refrigerators well enough, **monsieur.** Think about the aesthetics. You have to adjust constantly.
Oui, Chef!

Green Beans, White Peach,
and Fresh Almonds

Strawberries Sprinkled with
Crushed Berlingots and Olive Oil

Green Beans, White Peach, and Fresh Almonds

SERVES 4

Before I cook a recipe, I love to make a bouquet with the vegetables or fruit or both, such as the ingredients for this dish—green beans, white peach, and freshly shelled almonds. I arrange them on a plate like a still life, and I look at the interplay between their shapes and colors, thinking of the visual pleasure they will give.

In a large saucepan of rapidly boiling salted water, cook a bowl full of extra-thin green beans (**haricots verts**), uncovered, until al dente. Allow 3 minutes of cooking time, or 5 to 6 minutes for larger beans. With a skimmer, remove them from the saucepan, plunge in ice water, and drain on a kitchen towel. Place 3 tablespoons of salted butter in a large sauté pan over low heat and allow to melt and foam. Add the green beans and heat for 7 to 8 minutes, lifting them gently with a wooden spatula to stir. Now without stirring, so you won't damage the shapes, add 1 white peach, cut into matchsticks; 24 freshly shelled almonds; the juice of 1 lemon; 1 teaspoon of fresh thyme; and a bit of fleur de sel. Serve at once on warmed plates, carefully spooning up the tiny bit of sauce at the bottom of the sauté pan, which is a blend of butter and lemon juice.

Dip the green beans into ice water to stop the cooking process and preserve their bright color.

To make sure your white peach matchsticks will stay firm, choose a fruit that is not too ripe.

I like to flavor this with a few turns of black pepper; it imparts a delicious smoky flavor to the green beans and peach.

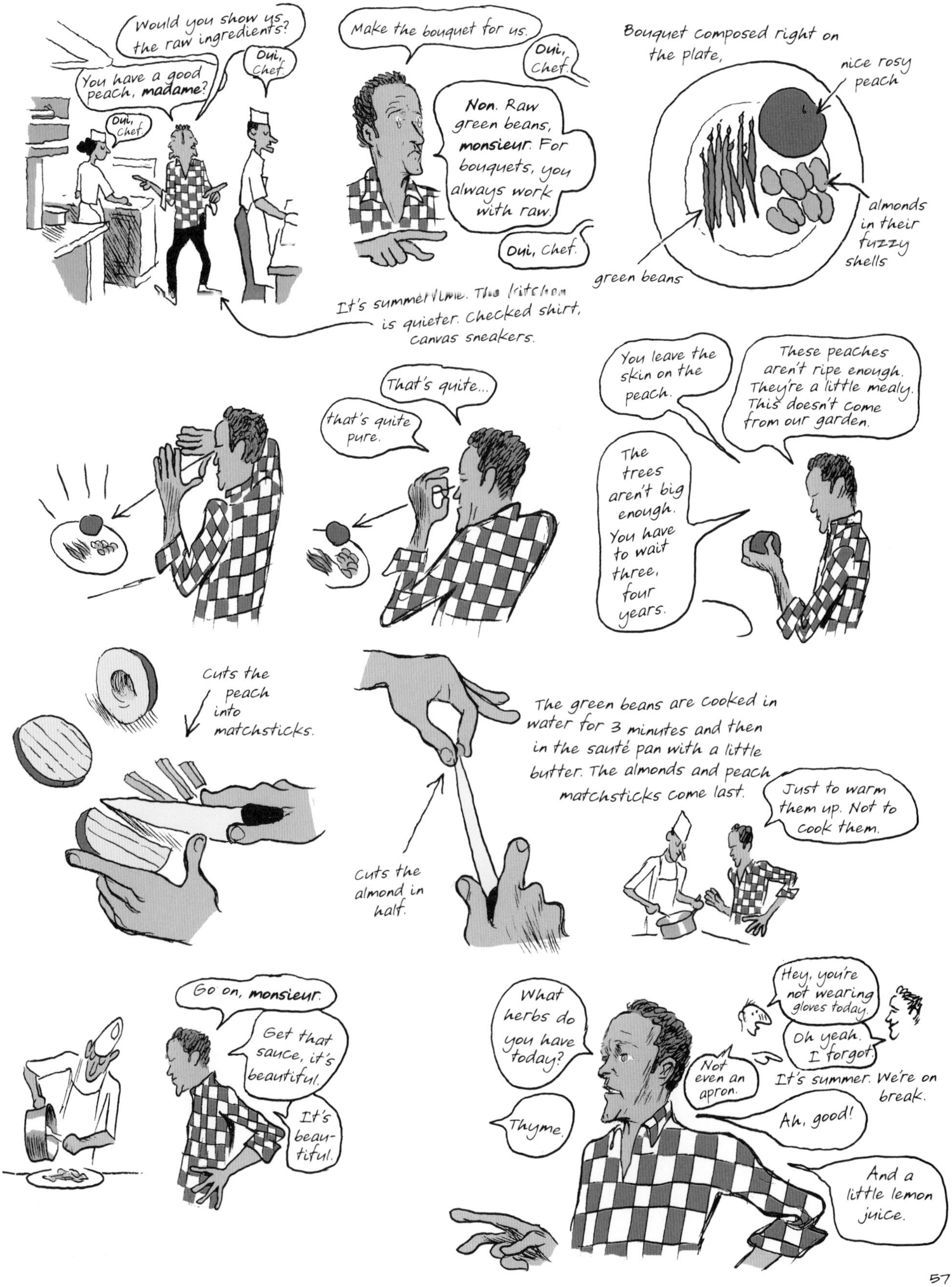

Would you show us the raw ingredients?
You have a good peach, **madame**?
Oui, Chef.
Oui, Chef.
It's summertime. The kitchen is quieter. Checked shirt, canvas sneakers.
Make the bouquet for us.
Oui, Chef.
Non. Raw green beans, **monsieur**. For bouquets, you always work with raw.
Oui, Chef.
Bouquet composed right on the plate,
nice rosy peach
almonds in their fuzzy shells
green beans
That's quite...
that's quite pure.
You leave the skin on the peach.
These peaches aren't ripe enough. They're a little mealy. This doesn't come from our garden.
The trees aren't big enough. You have to wait three, four years.
Cuts the peach into matchsticks.
Cuts the almond in half.
The green beans are cooked in water for 3 minutes and then in the sauté pan with a little butter. The almonds and peach matchsticks come last.
Just to warm them up. Not to cook them.
Go on, **monsieur**.
Get that sauce, it's beautiful.
It's beautiful.
What herbs do you have today?
Thyme.
Hey, you're not wearing gloves today.
Oh yeah. I forgot.
Not even an apron.
It's summer. We're on break.
Ah, good!
And a little lemon juice.

Strawberries Sprinkled with Crushed Berlingots and Olive Oil

SERVES 4

Slice 14 ounces of large strawberries (at room temperature) lengthwise. Arrange them on plates, sprinkle with crushed berlingot* candies, and dab the plate with a few drops of olive oil. Serve immediately. You can also accompany it with a bowl of pistachio ice cream and little palmiers, for a more indulgent dessert.

*See page 53.

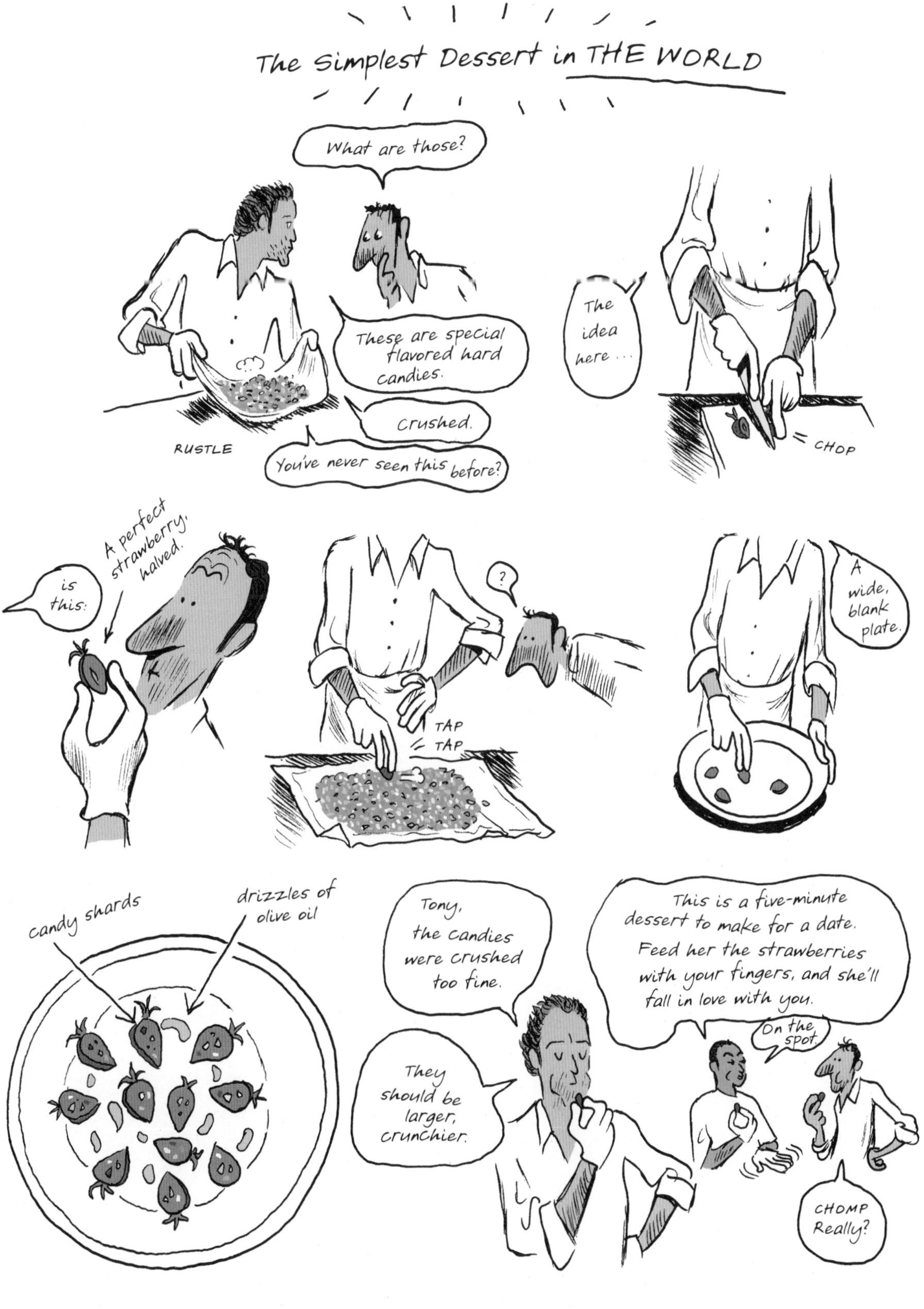

The Simplest Dessert in THE WORLD
What are those?
These are special flavored hard candies.
Crushed.
RUSTLE
You've never seen this before?
The idea here . . .
CHOP
is this:
A perfect strawberry, halved.
?
TAP
TAP
A wide, blank plate.
candy shards
drizzles of olive oil
Tony, the candies were crushed too fine.
They should be larger, crunchier.
This is a five-minute dessert to make for a date. Feed her the strawberries with your fingers, and she'll fall in love with you.
On the spot.
CHOMP
Really?

THE GARDEN IN NORMANDY

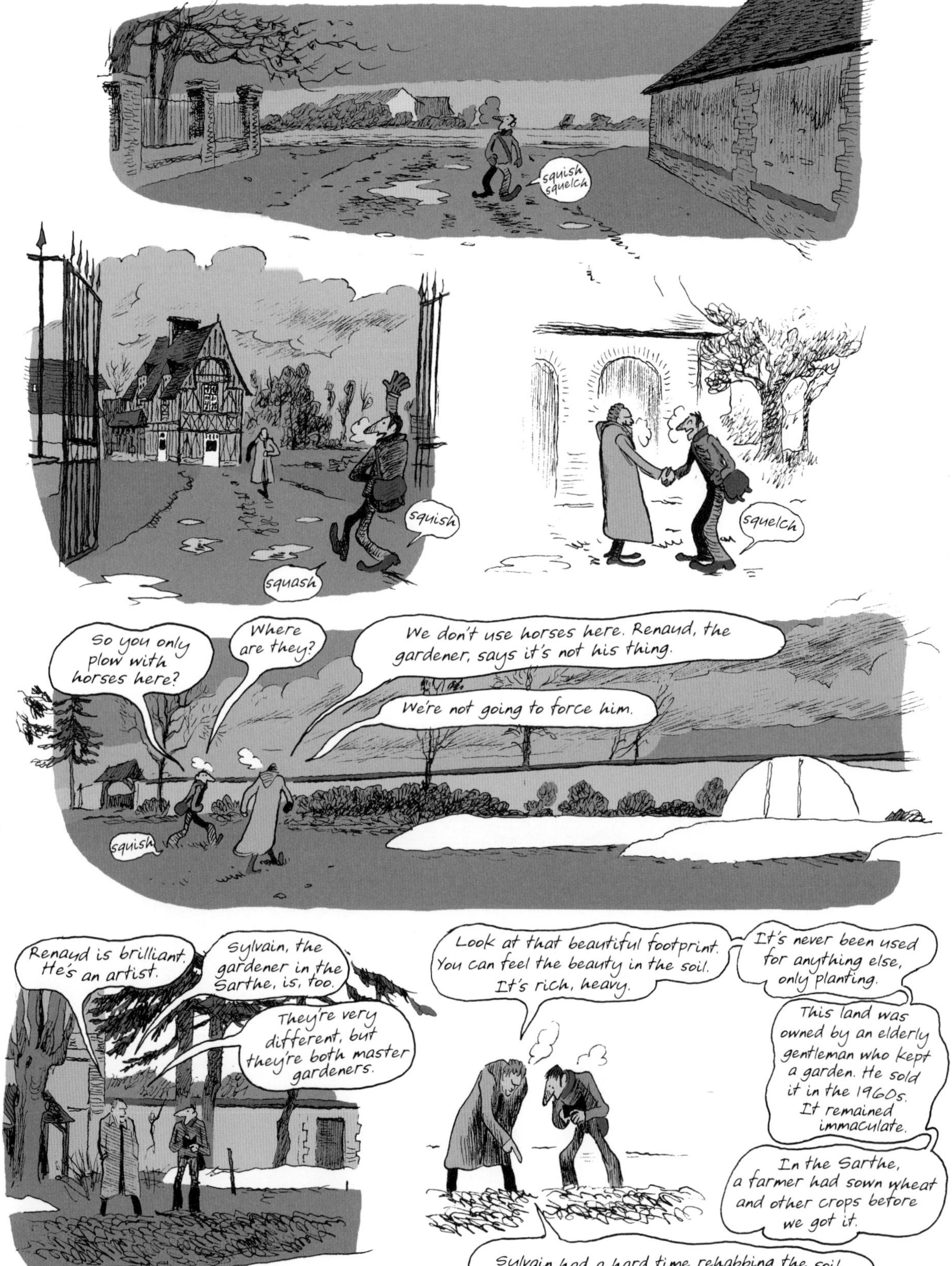
squish
squelch
squish
squash
squelch
So you only plow with horses here?
Where are they?
We don't use horses here. Renaud, the gardener, says it's not his thing.
We're not going to force him.
squish
Renaud is brilliant. He's an artist.
Sylvain, the gardener in the Sarthe, is, too.
They're very different, but they're both master gardeners.
Look at that beautiful footprint. You can feel the beauty in the soil. It's rich, heavy.
It's never been used for anything else, only planting.
This land was owned by an elderly gentleman who kept a garden. He sold it in the 1960s. It remained immaculate.
In the Sarthe, a farmer had sown wheat and other crops before we got it.
Sylvain had a hard time rehabbing the soil. Here it was prime and fertile.

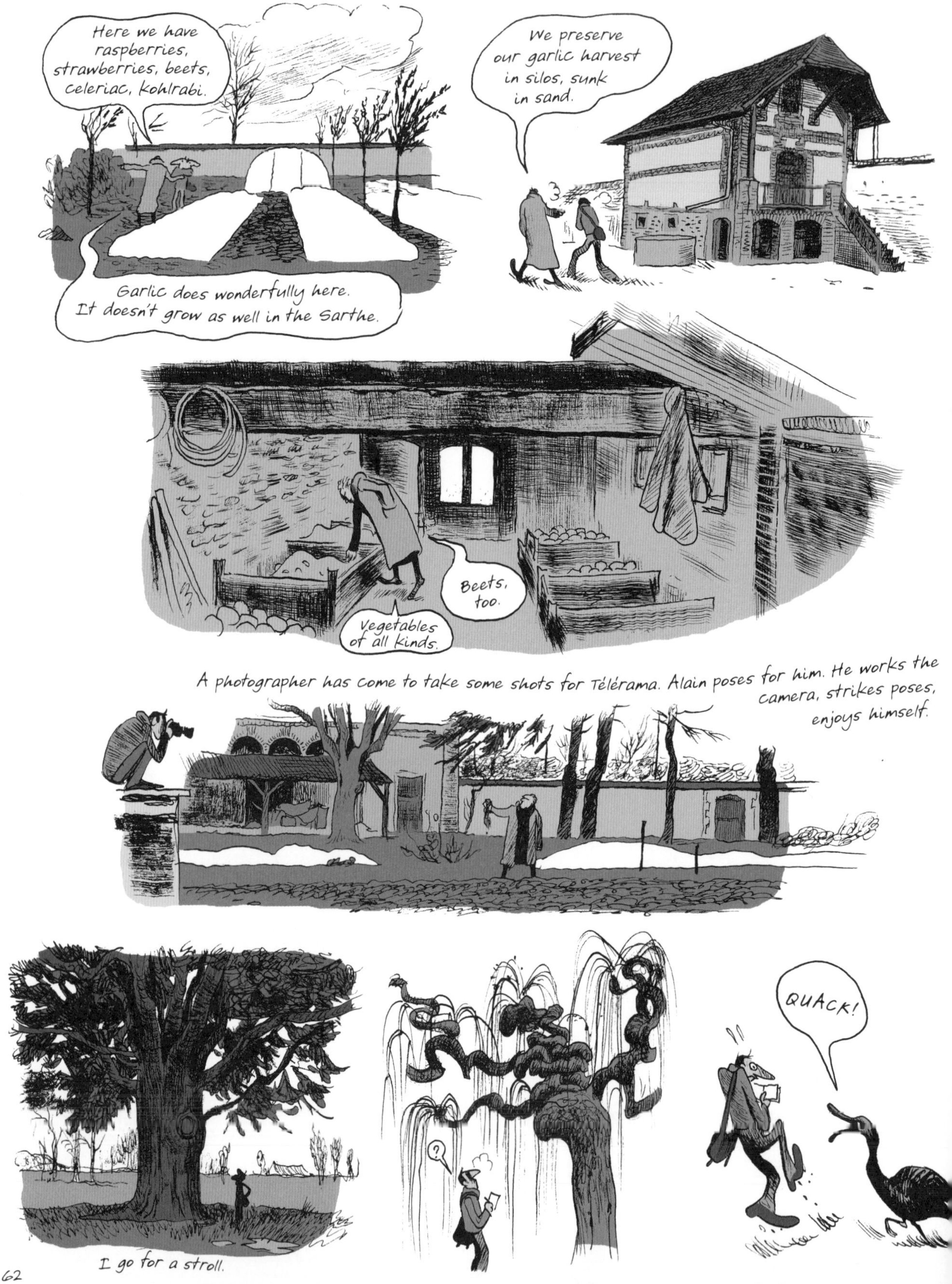
Here we have raspberries, strawberries, beets, celeriac, kohlrabi.
Garlic does wonderfully here. It doesn't grow as well in the Sarthe.
We preserve our garlic harvest in silos, sunk in sand.
Vegetables of all kinds.
Beets, too.
A photographer has come to take some shots for Télérama. Alain poses for him. He works the camera, strikes poses, enjoys himself.
I go for a stroll.
?
QUACK!

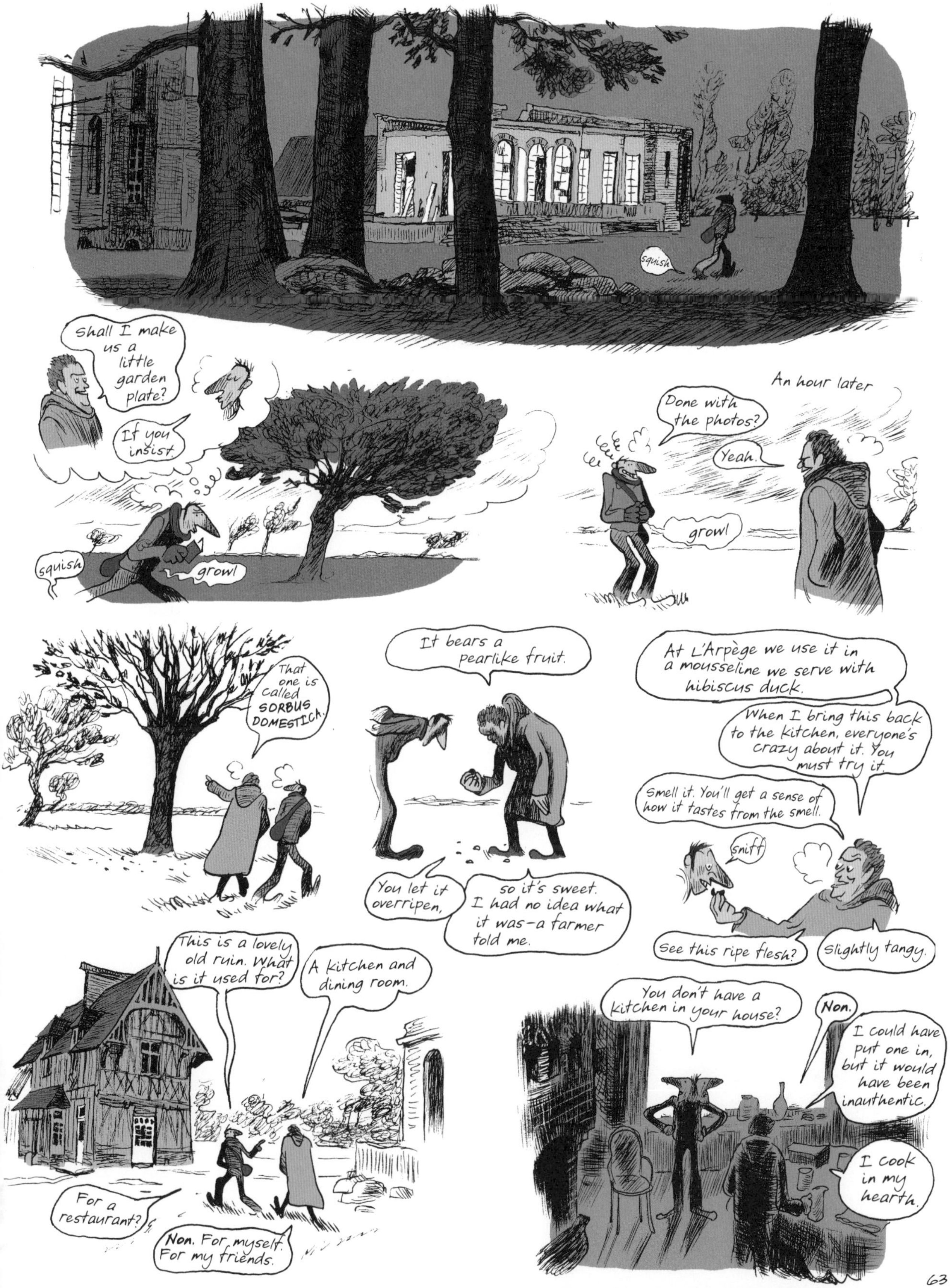
squish
Shall I make us a little garden plate?
If you insist.
squish
growl
An hour later
Done with the photos?
Yeah.
growl
That one is called SORBUS DOMESTICA.
It bears a pearlike fruit.
You let it overripen,
so it's sweet. I had no idea what it was—a farmer told me.
At L'Arpège we use it in a mousseline we serve with hibiscus duck.
When I bring this back to the kitchen, everyone's crazy about it. You must try it.
Smell it. You'll get a sense of how it tastes from the smell.
sniff
See this ripe flesh?
Slightly tangy.
This is a lovely old ruin. What is it used for?
A kitchen and dining room.
For a restaurant?
Non. For myself. For my friends.
You don't have a kitchen in your house?
Non.
I could have put one in, but it would have been inauthentic.
I cook in my hearth.

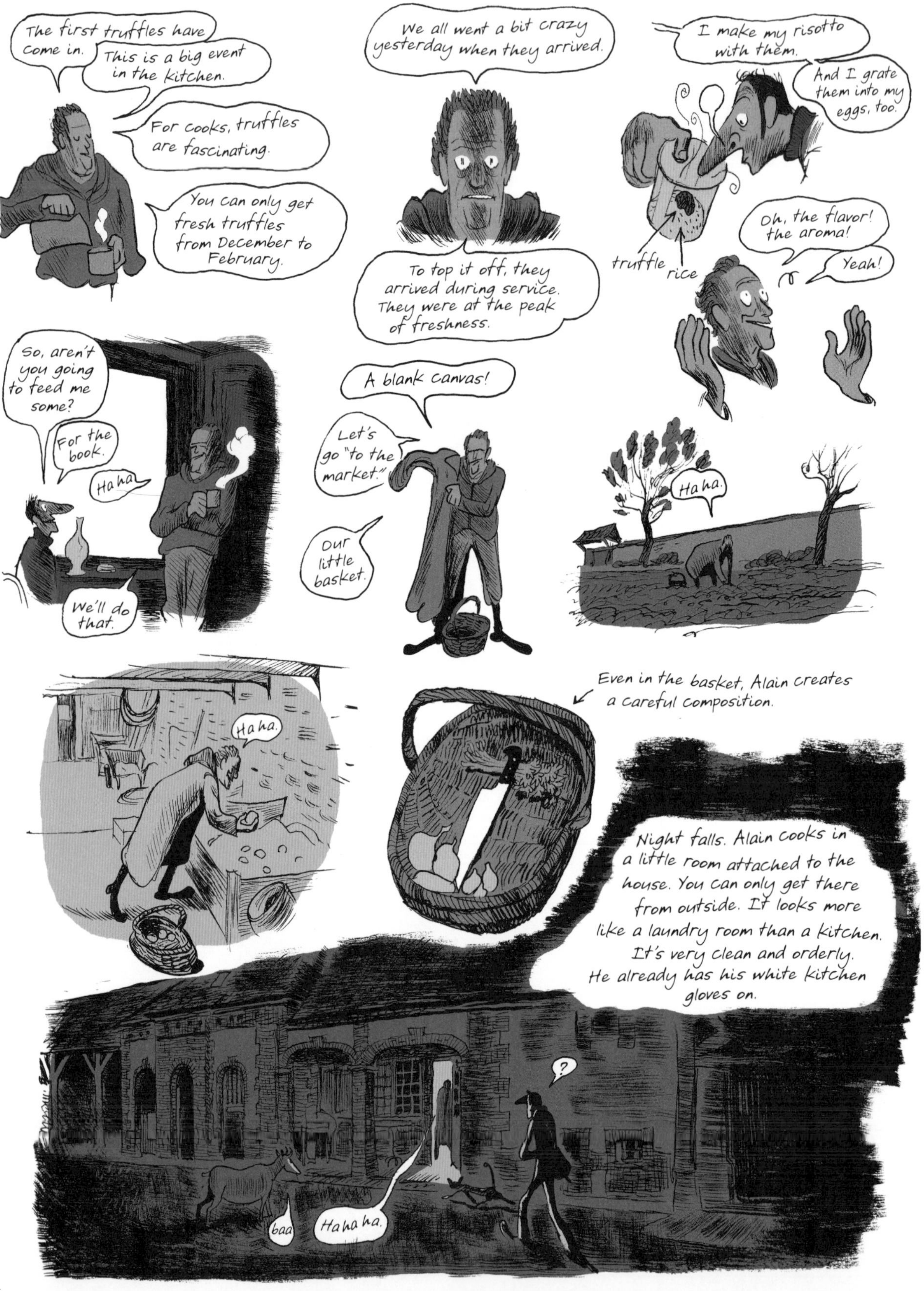
The first truffles have come in.
This is a big event in the kitchen.
For cooks, truffles are fascinating.
You can only get fresh truffles from December to February.
We all went a bit crazy yesterday when they arrived.
To top it off, they arrived during service. They were at the peak of freshness.
I make my risotto with them.
And I grate them into my eggs, too.
truffle
rice
Oh, the flavor! the aroma!
Yeah!
So, aren't you going to feed me some?
For the book.
Haha
We'll do that.
A blank canvas!
Let's go "to the market."
Our little basket.
Haha.
Haha.
Even in the basket, Alain creates a careful composition.
Night falls. Alain cooks in a little room attached to the house. You can only get there from outside. It looks more like a laundry room than a kitchen. It's very clean and orderly. He already has his white kitchen gloves on.
?
baa
Hahaha.

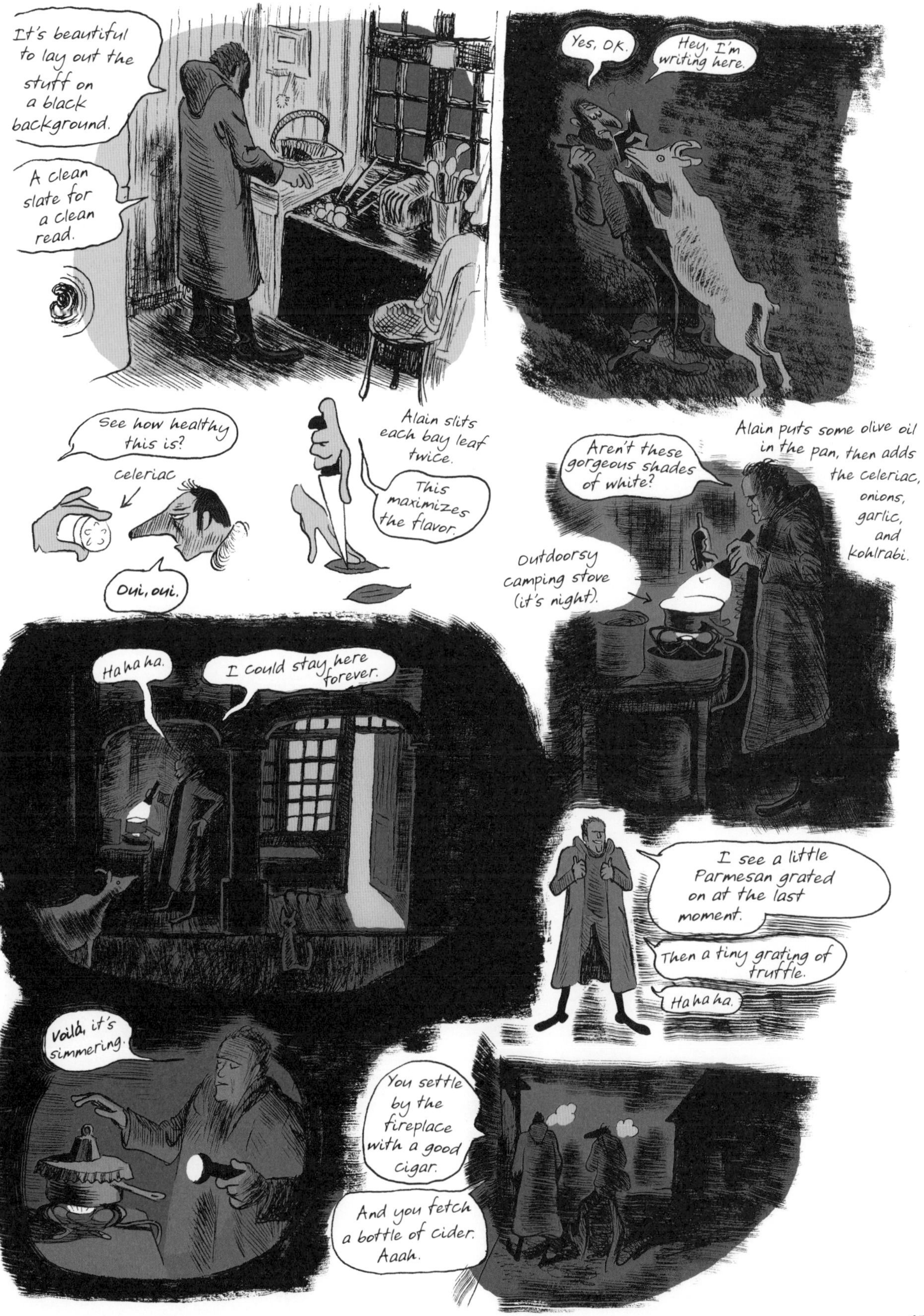
It's beautiful to lay out the stuff on a black background.
A clean slate for a clean read.
Yes, OK.
Hey, I'm writing here.
See how healthy this is?
celeriac
Oui, oui.
Alain slits each bay leaf twice.
This maximizes the flavor.
Aren't these gorgeous shades of white?
Alain puts some olive oil in the pan, then adds the celeriac, onions, garlic, and kohlrabi.
Outdoorsy camping stove (it's night).
Ha ha ha.
I could stay here forever.
I see a little Parmesan grated on at the last moment.
Then a tiny grating of truffle.
Ha ha ha.
Voilà, it's simmering.
You settle by the fireplace with a good cigar.
And you fetch a bottle of cider. Aaah.

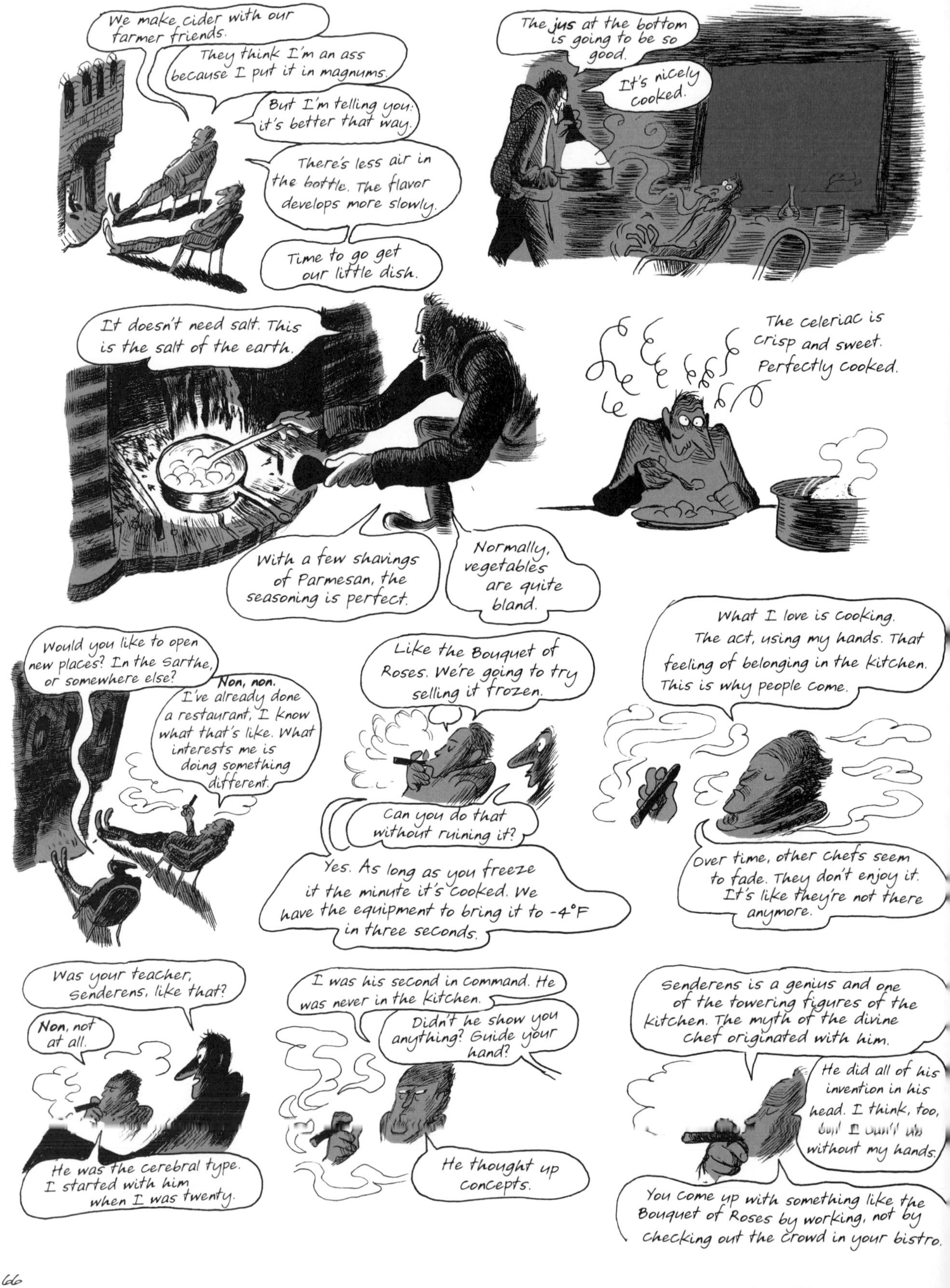
We make cider with our farmer friends.
They think I'm an ass because I put it in magnums.
But I'm telling you: it's better that way.
There's less air in the bottle. The flavor develops more slowly.
Time to go get our little dish.
The **jus** at the bottom is going to be so good.
It's nicely cooked.
It doesn't need salt. This is the salt of the earth.
With a few shavings of Parmesan, the seasoning is perfect.
Normally, vegetables are quite bland.
The celeriac is crisp and sweet. Perfectly cooked.
Would you like to open new places? In the Sarthe, or somewhere else?
Non, non. I've already done a restaurant, I know what that's like. What interests me is doing something different.
Like the Bouquet of Roses. We're going to try selling it frozen.
Can you do that without ruining it?
Yes. As long as you freeze it the minute it's cooked. We have the equipment to bring it to -4°F in three seconds.
What I love is cooking. The act, using my hands. That feeling of belonging in the kitchen. This is why people come.
Over time, other chefs seem to fade. They don't enjoy it. It's like they're not there anymore.
Was your teacher, Senderens, like that?
Non, not at all.
He was the cerebral type. I started with him when I was twenty.
I was his second in command. He was never in the kitchen.
Didn't he show you anything? Guide your hand?
He thought up concepts.
Senderens is a genius and one of the towering figures of the kitchen. The myth of the divine chef originated with him.
He did all of his invention in his head. I think, too, without my hands.
You come up with something like the Bouquet of Roses by working, not by checking out the crowd in your bistro.

Squab Dragée with Mead

Squab Dragée with Mead

SERVES 4

In a frying pan, cook 2 young squabs, turning them often, for 45 minutes. I'm fond of this method of cooking, where you see what you're working with and hear it cooking. Squab is a very delicate fowl with silky flesh. In the oven it would reach the designated temperature and become dehydrated. But what I find worse is the closed oven door! I can't hear anything or see anything that way, and when I cook I need to gather information with all my senses: visual, auditory, tactile, and olfactory. Voilà, that's my little lecture on choosing the right type of heat.

In a sauté pan, over low heat, melt and lightly caramelize about 30 dragées* for 7 or 8 minutes, stirring occasionally. They will stick together in a mass; that's OK. Turn off the heat and let them cool in the pan. With a rolling pin, crush the block of dragées until they are the texture of somewhat coarse bread crumbs.

Now, in the frying pan, slick the cooked squabs with a chunk of salted butter until they have a nice sheen, then coat them all over with some of the crushed dragées. Under a preheated broiler, caramelize the birds' skin; the melding of the salted butter and the sugar from the dragées will impart a lovely golden color. A small amount of blood will escape. Leave this in the pan, as it will be used to flavor and thicken the sauce.

Arrange the squabs on a platter, season with fleur de sel and quatre épices (see page 40), and show the birds to your guests. Return the squabs to the kitchen. In the frying pan with the squab blood, caramelize ¼ cup of the dragée crumbs over low heat with 2 chips of salted butter for 2 to 3 minutes. Add 1 cup of mead and a ladle full of water, and simmer—while your guests are raving about your cooking! Carve the squabs, separating the flesh from the carcasses. Chop the carcasses into large pieces and add to the simmering mead along with 2 chopped squab livers and ½ lemon, sliced into thin rounds. Stir the sauce and add what I call the "carving juice"—the liquid left on your work surface after you have carved the squabs. Your sauce should be thick enough to coat the back of a spoon and have a nice sheen. Run it through a chinois (a conical sieve); push hard to get every drop. Correct the seasoning and serve steaming hot with the four squab halves. Be sure to warm your plates, and garnish with endive leaves grilled or sautéed in salted butter.

*Dragées are candied almonds.

This recipe can also be used for ducklings or even, in hunting season, wild duck.

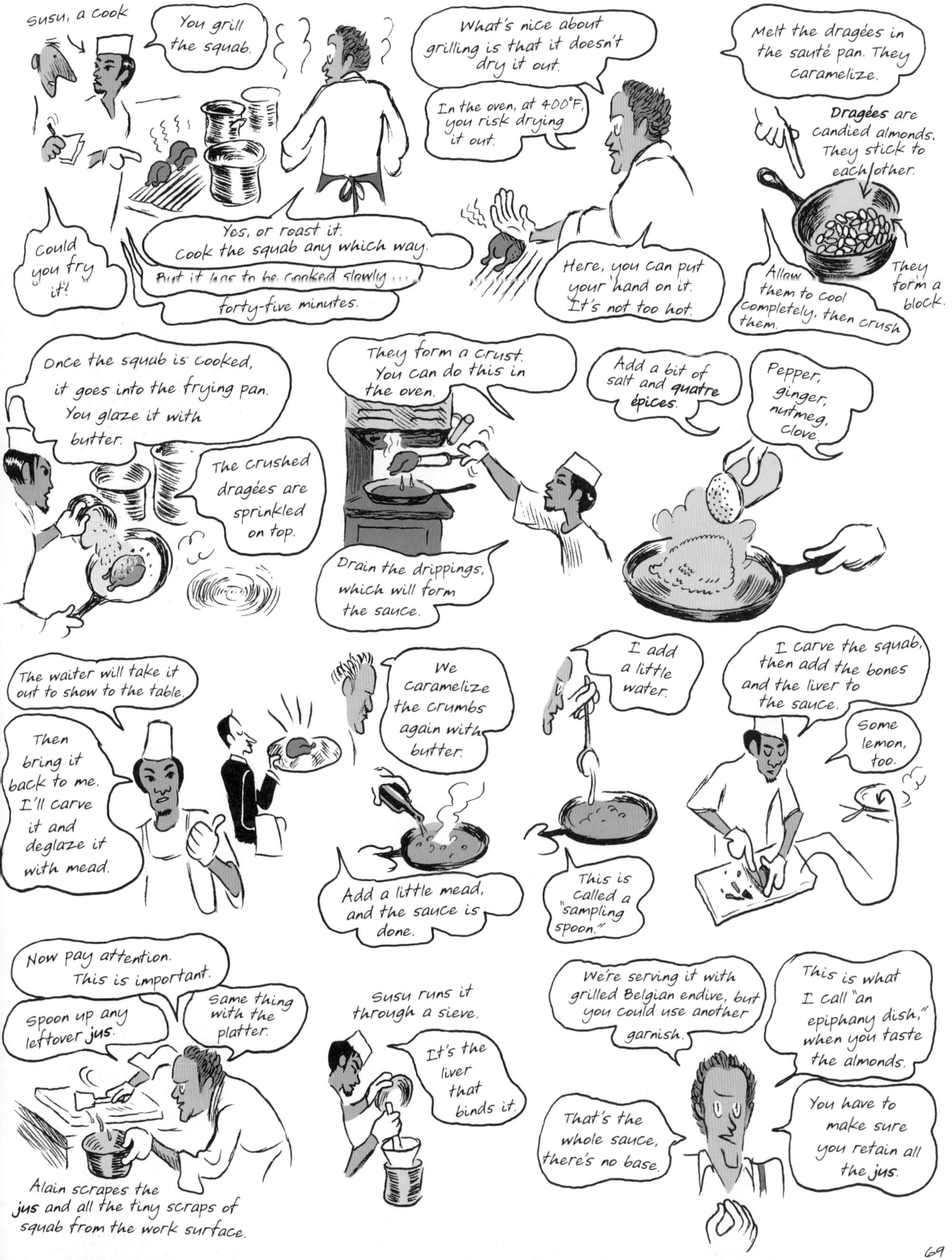
Susu, a cook
You grill the squab.
Could you fry it?
Yes, or roast it. Cook the squab any which way.
But it has to be cooked slowly . . .
forty-five minutes.
What's nice about grilling is that it doesn't dry it out.
In the oven, at 400°F, you risk drying it out.
Here, you can put your hand on it. It's not too hot.
Melt the dragées in the sauté pan. They caramelize.
Dragées are candied almonds. They stick to each other.
They form a block.
Allow them to cool completely, then crush them.
Once the squab is cooked, it goes into the frying pan. You glaze it with butter.
The crushed dragées are sprinkled on top.
They form a crust. You can do this in the oven.
Drain the drippings, which will form the sauce.
Add a bit of salt and **quatre épices**.
Pepper, ginger, nutmeg, clove.
The waiter will take it out to show to the table.
Then bring it back to me. I'll carve it and deglaze it with mead.
We caramelize the crumbs again with butter.
Add a little mead, and the sauce is done.
I add a little water.
This is called a "sampling spoon."
I carve the squab, then add the bones and the liver to the sauce.
Some lemon, too.
Now pay attention. This is important.
Spoon up any leftover **jus**.
Same thing with the platter.
Alain scrapes the **jus** and all the tiny scraps of squab from the work surface.
Susu runs it through a sieve.
It's the liver that binds it.
We're serving it with grilled Belgian endive, but you could use another garnish.
That's the whole sauce, there's no base.
This is what I call "an epiphany dish," when you taste the almonds.
You have to make sure you retain all the **jus**.

THE GARDEN IN THE SARTHE

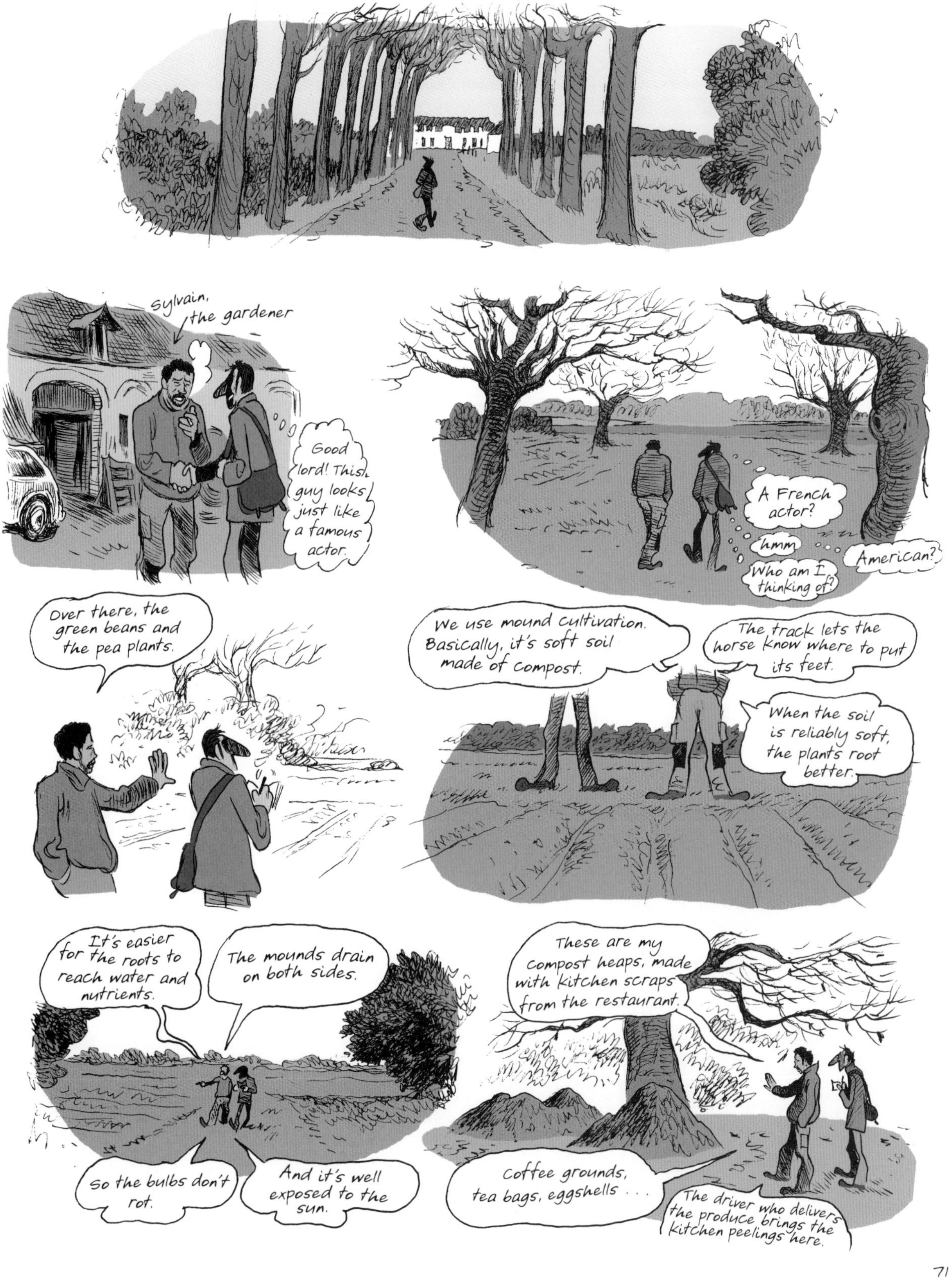
Sylvain, the gardener
Good lord! This guy looks just like a famous actor.
A French actor?
hmm
Who am I thinking of?
American?
Over there, the green beans and the pea plants.
We use mound cultivation. Basically, it's soft soil made of compost.
The track lets the horse know where to put its feet.
When the soil is reliably soft, the plants root better.
It's easier for the roots to reach water and nutrients.
The mounds drain on both sides.
So the bulbs don't rot.
And it's well exposed to the sun.
These are my compost heaps, made with kitchen scraps from the restaurant.
Coffee grounds, tea bags, eggshells . . .
The driver who delivers the produce brings the kitchen peelings here.

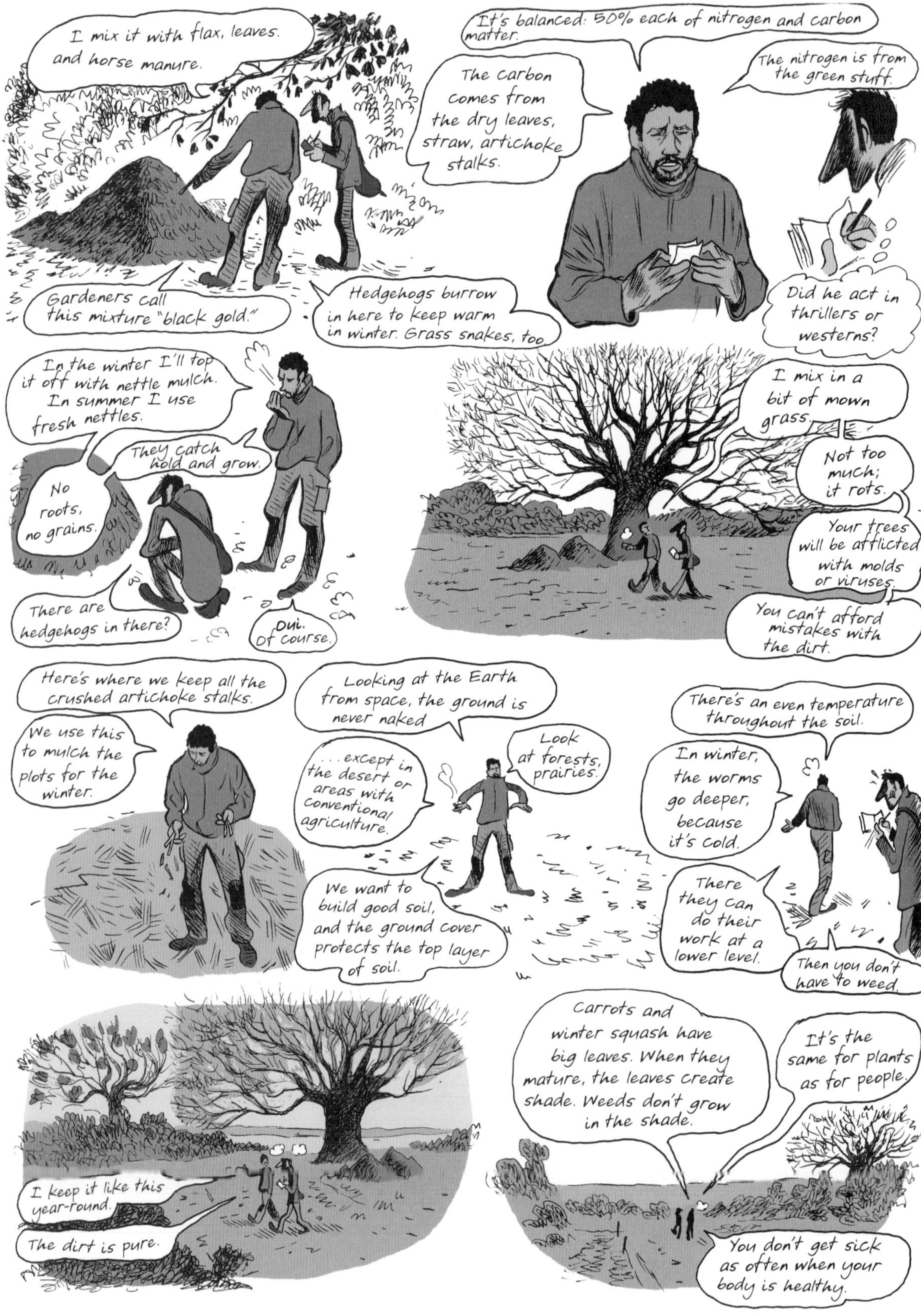
I mix it with flax, leaves. and horse manure.
Gardeners call this mixture "black gold."
Hedgehogs burrow in here to keep warm in winter. Grass snakes, too.
It's balanced: 50% each of nitrogen and carbon matter.
The carbon comes from the dry leaves, straw, artichoke stalks.
The nitrogen is from the green stuff.
Did he act in thrillers or westerns?
In the winter I'll top it off with nettle mulch. In summer I use fresh nettles.
They catch hold and grow.
No roots, no grains.
There are hedgehogs in there?
Oui. Of course.
I mix in a bit of mown grass.
Not too much; it rots.
Your trees will be afflicted with molds or viruses.
You can't afford mistakes with the dirt.
Here's where we keep all the crushed artichoke stalks.
We use this to mulch the plots for the winter.
Looking at the Earth from space, the ground is never naked
...except in the desert or areas with conventional agriculture.
Look at forests, prairies.
We want to build good soil, and the ground cover protects the top layer of soil.
There's an even temperature throughout the soil.
In winter, the worms go deeper, because it's cold.
There they can do their work at a lower level.
Then you don't have to weed.
I keep it like this year-round.
The dirt is pure.
Carrots and winter squash have big leaves. When they mature, the leaves create shade. Weeds don't grow in the shade.
It's the same for plants as for people.
You don't get sick as often when your body is healthy.

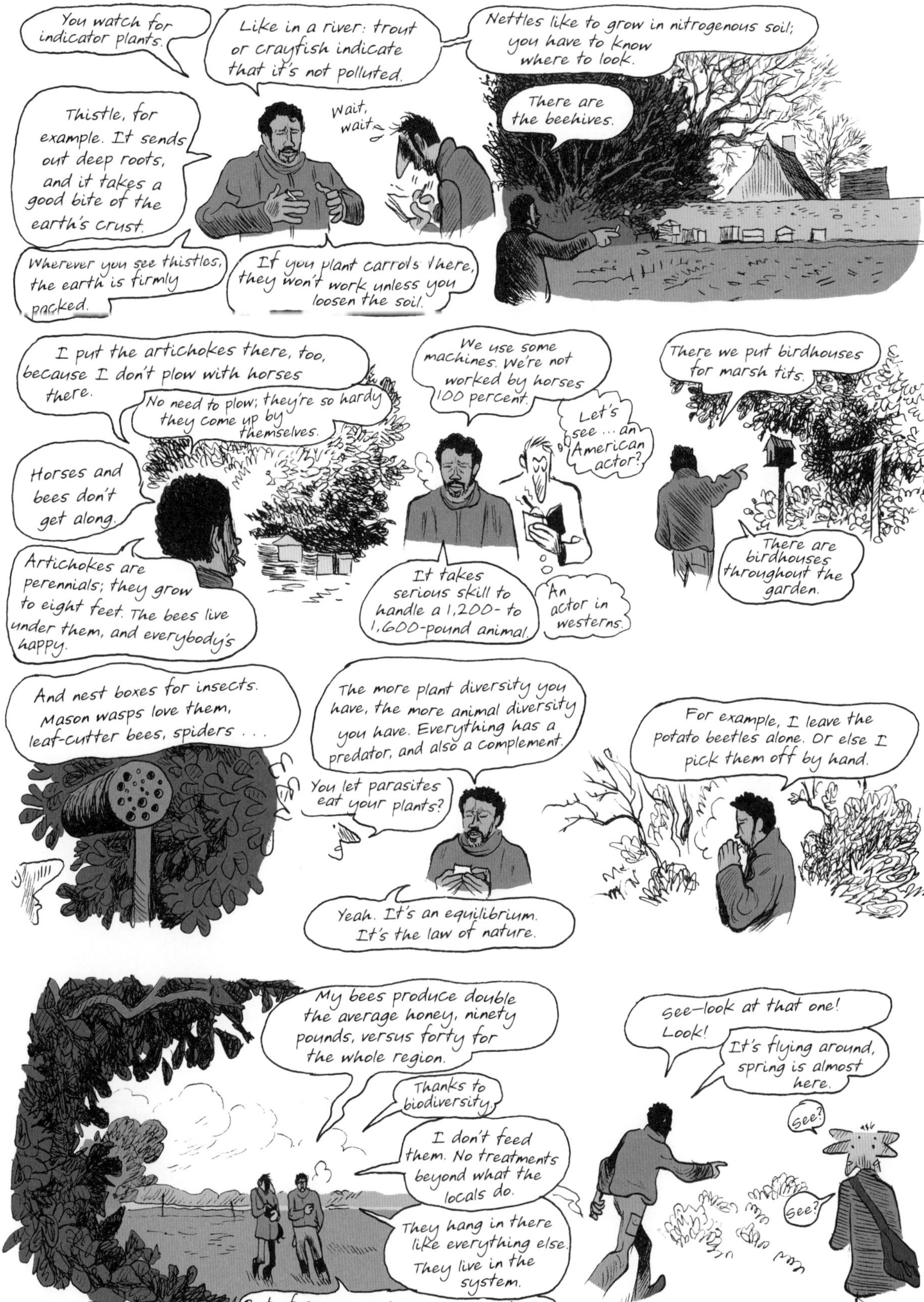

You watch for indicator plants.
Like in a river: trout or crayfish indicate that it's not polluted.
Nettles like to grow in nitrogenous soil; you have to know where to look.
Thistle, for example. It sends out deep roots, and it takes a good bite of the earth's crust.
Wait, wait
Wherever you see thistles, the earth is firmly packed.
If you plant carrots there, they won't work unless you loosen the soil.
There are the beehives.
I put the artichokes there, too, because I don't plow with horses there.
No need to plow; they're so hardy they come up by themselves.
Horses and bees don't get along.
Artichokes are perennials; they grow to eight feet. The bees live under them, and everybody's happy.
We use some machines. We're not worked by horses 100 percent.
Let's see . . . an American actor?
It takes serious skill to handle a 1,200- to 1,600-pound animal.
An actor in westerns.
There we put birdhouses for marsh tits.
There are birdhouses throughout the garden.
And nest boxes for insects. Mason wasps love them, leaf-cutter bees, spiders . . .
The more plant diversity you have, the more animal diversity you have. Everything has a predator, and also a complement.
You let parasites eat your plants?
Yeah. It's an equilibrium. It's the law of nature.
For example, I leave the potato beetles alone. Or else I pick them off by hand.
My bees produce double the average honey, ninety pounds, versus forty for the whole region.
Thanks to biodiversity.
I don't feed them. No treatments beyond what the locals do.
They hang in there like everything else. They live in the system.
But of course, I keep an eye on them.
See—look at that one! Look!
It's flying around, spring is almost here.
See?
See?

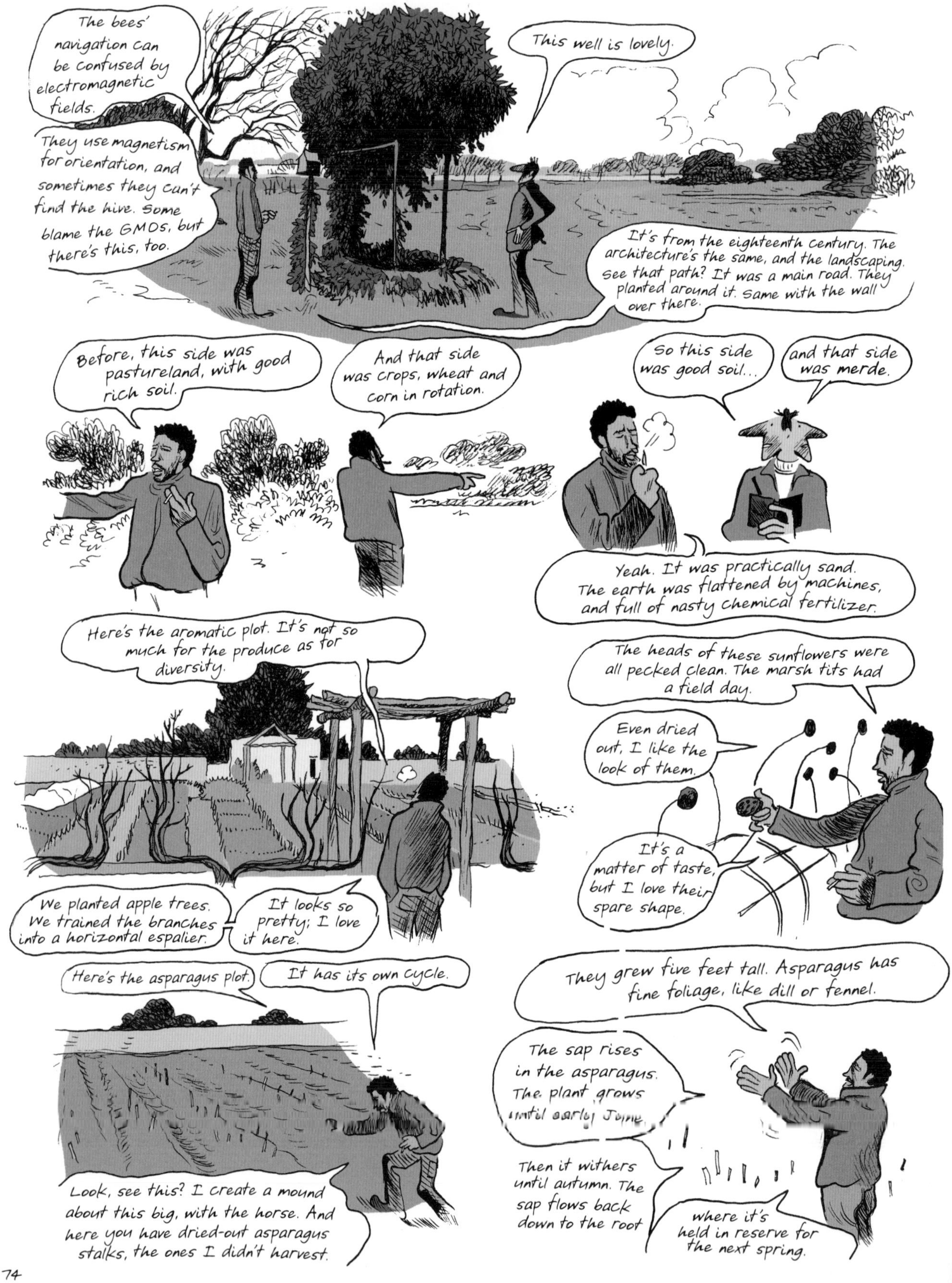
The bees' navigation can be confused by electromagnetic fields.
They use magnetism for orientation, and sometimes they can't find the hive. Some blame the GMOs, but there's this, too.
This well is lovely.
It's from the eighteenth century. The architecture's the same, and the landscaping. See that path? It was a main road. They planted around it. Same with the wall over there.
Before, this side was pastureland, with good rich soil.
And that side was crops, wheat and corn in rotation.
So this side was good soil...
and that side was merde.
Yeah. It was practically sand. The earth was flattened by machines, and full of nasty chemical fertilizer.
Here's the aromatic plot. It's not so much for the produce as for diversity.
We planted apple trees. We trained the branches into a horizontal espalier.
It looks so pretty; I love it here.
The heads of these sunflowers were all pecked clean. The marsh tits had a field day.
Even dried out, I like the look of them.
It's a matter of taste, but I love their spare shape.
Here's the asparagus plot.
It has its own cycle.
Look, see this? I create a mound about this big, with the horse. And here you have dried-out asparagus stalks, the ones I didn't harvest.
They grew five feet tall. Asparagus has fine foliage, like dill or fennel.
The sap rises in the asparagus. The plant grows until early June.
Then it withers until autumn. The sap flows back down to the root
where it's held in reserve for the next spring.

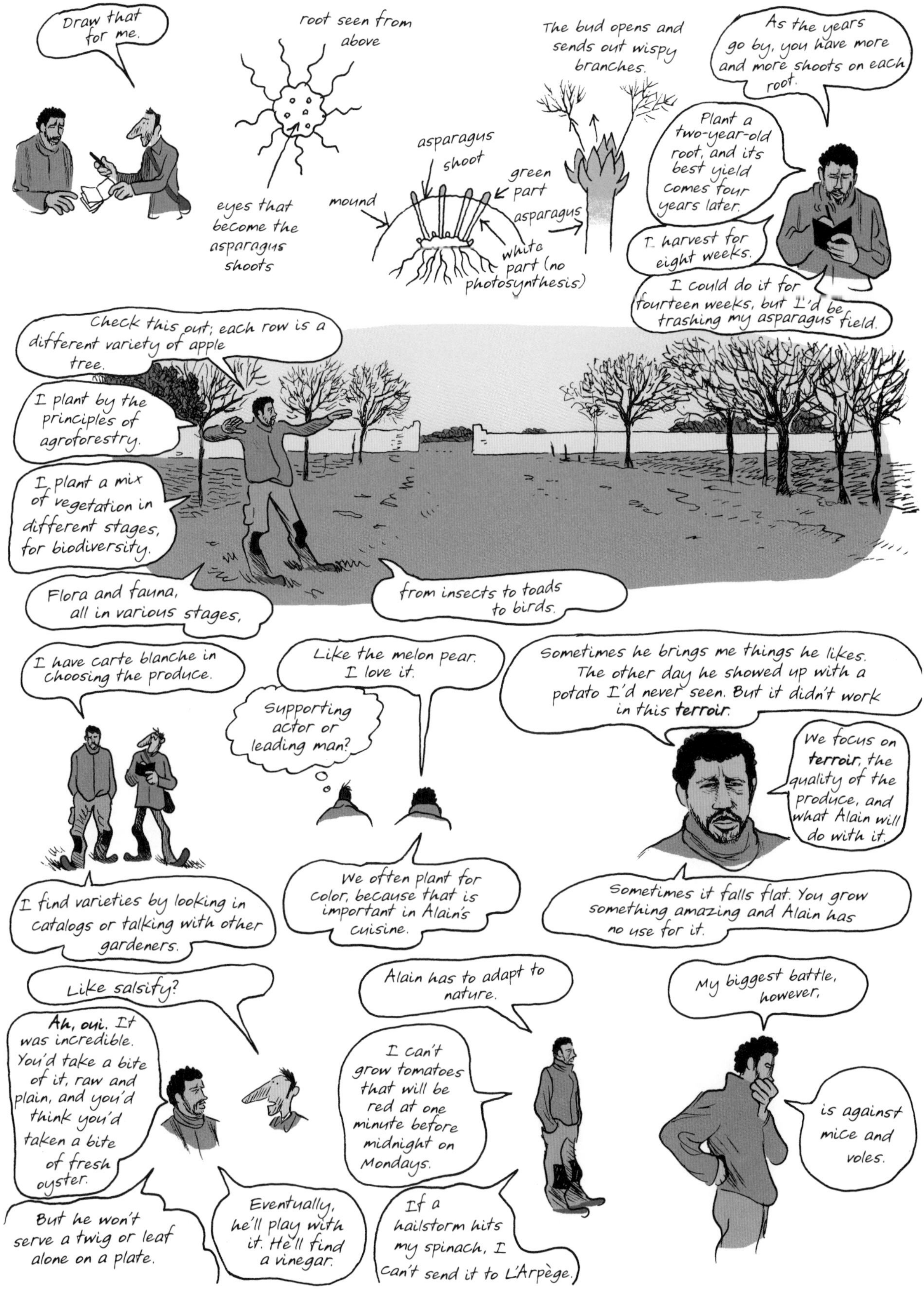
Draw that for me.
root seen from above
eyes that become the asparagus shoots
asparagus shoot
mound
green part
asparagus
white part (no photosynthesis)
The bud opens and sends out wispy branches.
As the years go by, you have more and more shoots on each root.
Plant a two-year-old root, and its best yield comes four years later.
I harvest for eight weeks.
I could do it for fourteen weeks, but I'd be trashing my asparagus field.
Check this out; each row is a different variety of apple tree.
I plant by the principles of agroforestry.
I plant a mix of vegetation in different stages, for biodiversity.
Flora and fauna, all in various stages,
from insects to toads to birds.
I have carte blanche in choosing the produce.
I find varieties by looking in catalogs or talking with other gardeners.
Like the melon pear. I love it.
Supporting actor or leading man?
We often plant for color, because that is important in Alain's cuisine.
Sometimes he brings me things he likes. The other day he showed up with a potato I'd never seen. But it didn't work in this **terroir**.
We focus on **terroir**, the quality of the produce, and what Alain will do with it.
Sometimes it falls flat. You grow something amazing and Alain has no use for it.
Like salsify?
Ah, oui. It was incredible. You'd take a bite of it, raw and plain, and you'd think you'd taken a bite of fresh oyster.
But he won't serve a twig or leaf alone on a plate.
Eventually, he'll play with it. He'll find a vinegar.
Alain has to adapt to nature.
I can't grow tomatoes that will be red at one minute before midnight on Mondays.
If a hailstorm hits my spinach, I can't send it to L'Arpège.
My biggest battle, however,
is against mice and voles.

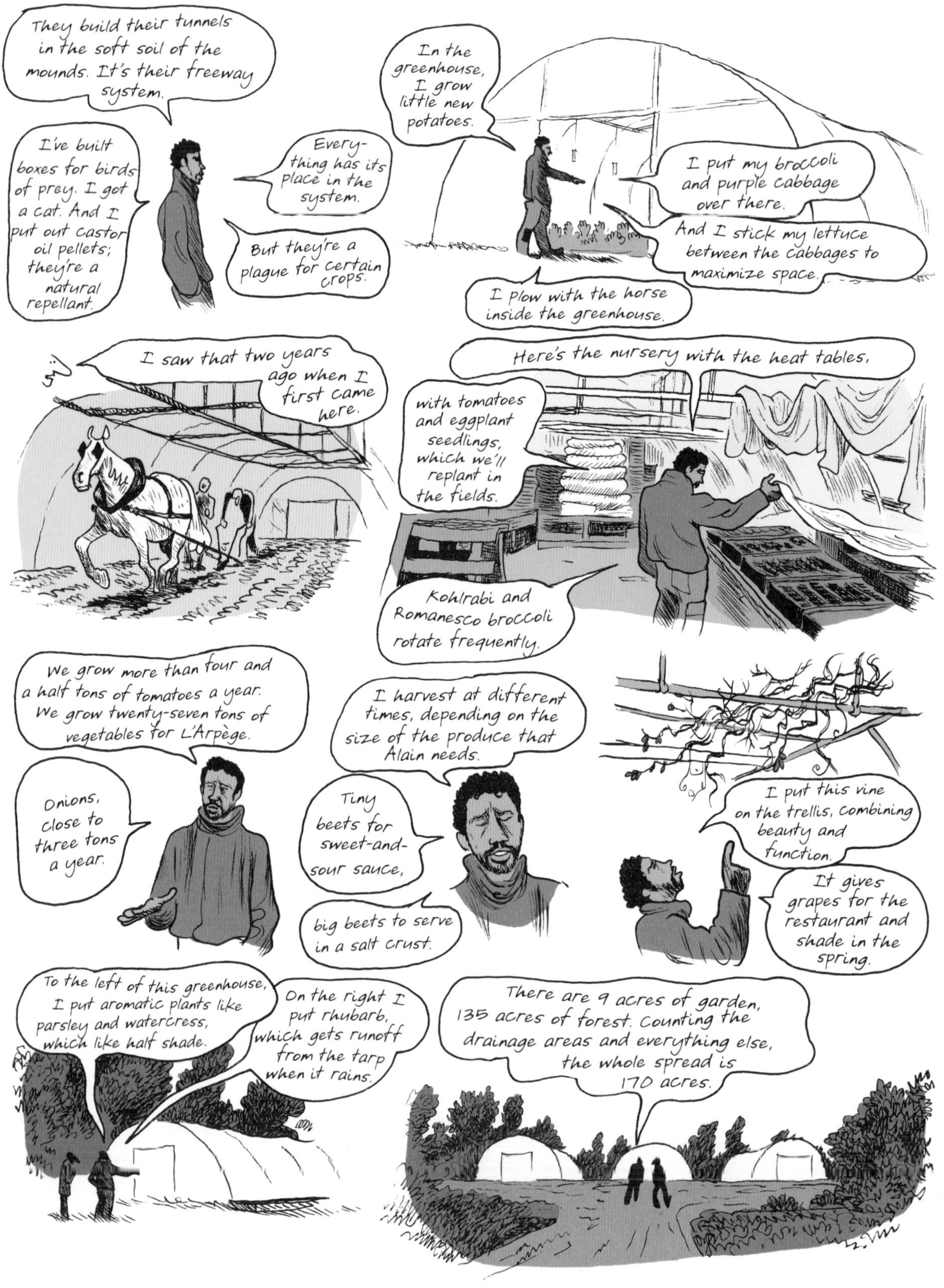
They build their tunnels in the soft soil of the mounds. It's their freeway system.
I've built boxes for birds of prey. I got a cat. And I put out castor oil pellets; they're a natural repellant.
Everything has its place in the system.
But they're a plague for certain crops.
In the greenhouse, I grow little new potatoes.
I put my broccoli and purple cabbage over there.
And I stick my lettuce between the cabbages to maximize space.
I plow with the horse inside the greenhouse.
I saw that two years ago when I first came here.
Here's the nursery with the heat tables,
with tomatoes and eggplant seedlings, which we'll replant in the fields.
Kohlrabi and Romanesco broccoli rotate frequently.
We grow more than four and a half tons of tomatoes a year. We grow twenty-seven tons of vegetables for L'Arpège.
Onions, close to three tons a year.
I harvest at different times, depending on the size of the produce that Alain needs.
Tiny beets for sweet-and-sour sauce,
big beets to serve in a salt crust.
I put this vine on the trellis, combining beauty and function.
It gives grapes for the restaurant and shade in the spring.
To the left of this greenhouse, I put aromatic plants like parsley and watercress, which like half shade.
On the right I put rhubarb, which gets runoff from the tarp when it rains.
There are 9 acres of garden, 135 acres of forest. Counting the drainage areas and everything else, the whole spread is 170 acres.

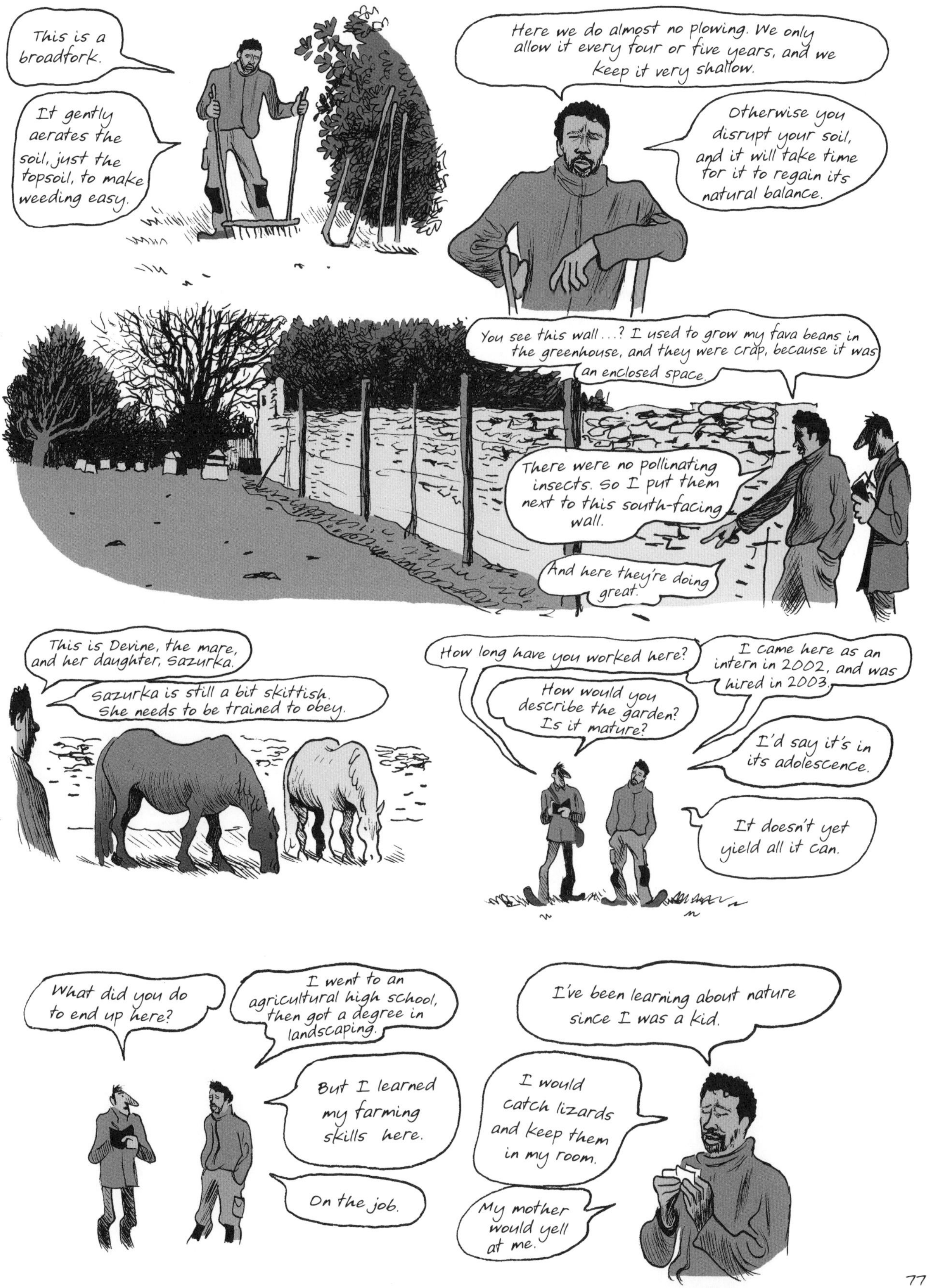

This is a broadfork.
It gently aerates the soil, just the topsoil, to make weeding easy.
Here we do almost no plowing. We only allow it every four or five years, and we keep it very shallow.
Otherwise you disrupt your soil, and it will take time for it to regain its natural balance.
You see this wall...? I used to grow my fava beans in the greenhouse, and they were crap, because it was an enclosed space.
There were no pollinating insects. So I put them next to this south-facing wall.
And here they're doing great.
This is Devine, the mare, and her daughter, Sazurka.
Sazurka is still a bit skittish. She needs to be trained to obey.
How long have you worked here?
I came here as an intern in 2002, and was hired in 2003.
How would you describe the garden? Is it mature?
I'd say it's in its adolescence.
It doesn't yet yield all it can.
What did you do to end up here?
I went to an agricultural high school, then got a degree in landscaping.
But I learned my farming skills here.
On the job.
I've been learning about nature since I was a kid.
I would catch lizards and keep them in my room.
My mother would yell at me.

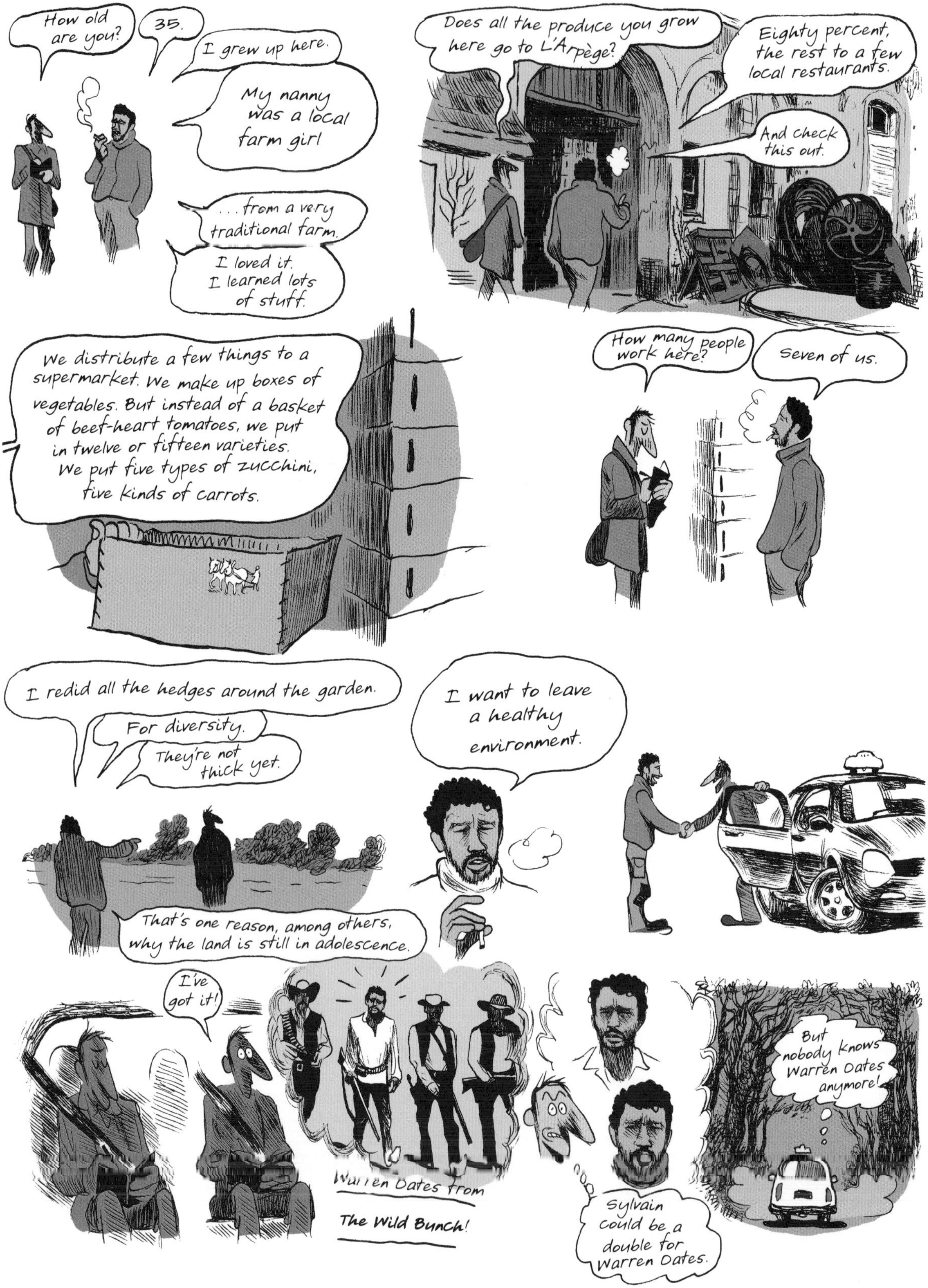
How old are you?
35.
I grew up here.
My nanny was a local farm girl
...from a very traditional farm.
I loved it. I learned lots of stuff.
Does all the produce you grow here go to L'Arpège?
Eighty percent, the rest to a few local restaurants.
And check this out.
We distribute a few things to a supermarket. We make up boxes of vegetables. But instead of a basket of beef-heart tomatoes, we put in twelve or fifteen varieties. We put five types of zucchini, five kinds of carrots.
How many people work here?
Seven of us.
I redid all the hedges around the garden.
For diversity.
They're not thick yet.
That's one reason, among others, why the land is still in adolescence.
I want to leave a healthy environment.
I've got it!
Warren Oates from
The Wild Bunch!
Sylvain could be a double for Warren Oates.
But nobody knows Warren Oates anymore!

Pineapple with Olive Oil, Honey, and Lemon

Pineapple with Olive Oil, Honey, and Lemon

SERVES 4

I like a pineapple with a light, luminous, flexible rind. The base, the tenderest and most flavorful part of the fruit, where the sugar is found, should give off exotic floral aromas. Choose a pineapple with colorful eyes ringed with a faint green border; pick by the freshness of the plume and peduncle, too. I recommend the Queen Victoria variety, a small pineapple with yellow skin; short, spiny leaves; soft, aromatic pulp; and abundant, very tasty juice. I also like the Smooth Cayenne variety, grown in all the major pineapple-producing countries and characterized by an almost thornless plume.

On your work space, place one 5-ounce pot of liquid acacia honey, 1 green apple, 1 cup of olive oil, 1 pineapple, and 2 limes. In a measuring cup, mix the honey with the juice of the limes. Add the olive oil to the honey-lime mixture, a little bit at a time, as though you were making mayonnaise. Skin the pineapple and cut it into ¾-inch cubes. Pool 4 to 5 tablespoons of the honey, lime, and olive oil emulsion on each plate. This is your base on which to build a little "castle" of 12 pineapple cubes per plate, topping each one with five or six "petals" of green apple, sliced on the mandoline at the last moment. Garnish with a sprinkling of fresh rosemary, snipped directly over the plates.

The lime juice can be replaced by lemon juice, and the olive oil by peanut oil.

In summer, this recipe is delicious with large garden strawberries and fresh white peach quarters.

This is totally unrelated, but I love leeks and baby potatoes, with skins on, cooked in water and tossed in this vinaigrette. Ha ha ha!

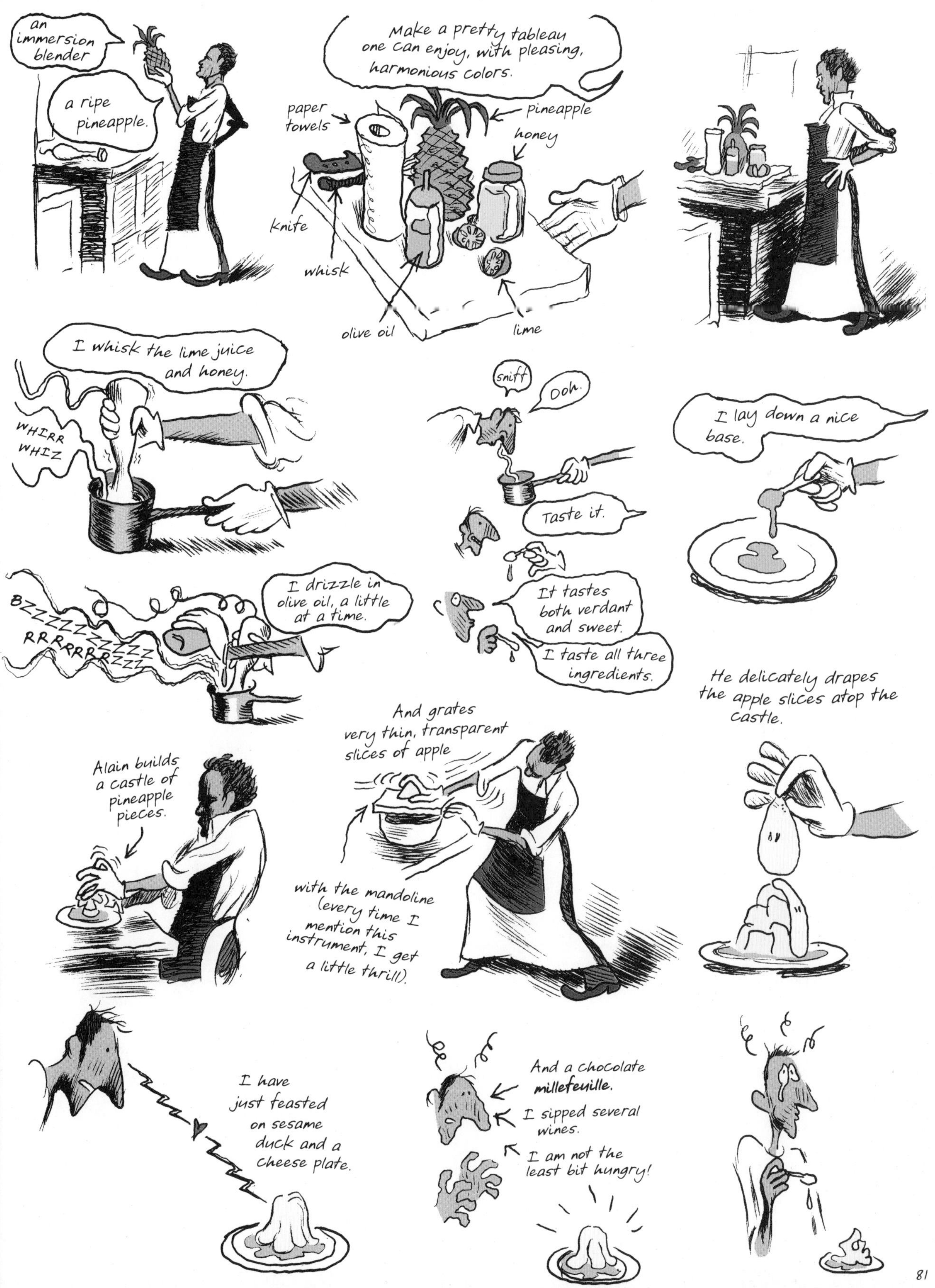
an immersion blender
a ripe pineapple.
Make a pretty tableau one can enjoy, with pleasing, harmonious colors.
paper towels
pineapple
honey
knife
whisk
olive oil
lime
I whisk the lime juice and honey.
WHIRR WHIZ
sniff
Ooh.
Taste it.
I lay down a nice base.
BZZZZZZZZZZZ RRRRRRRZZZZ
I drizzle in olive oil, a little at a time.
It tastes both verdant and sweet.
I taste all three ingredients.
He delicately drapes the apple slices atop the castle.
Alain builds a castle of pineapple pieces.
And grates very thin, transparent slices of apple
with the mandoline (every time I mention this instrument, I get a little thrill).
I have just feasted on sesame duck and a cheese plate.
And a chocolate millefeuille.
I sipped several wines.
I am not the least bit hungry!

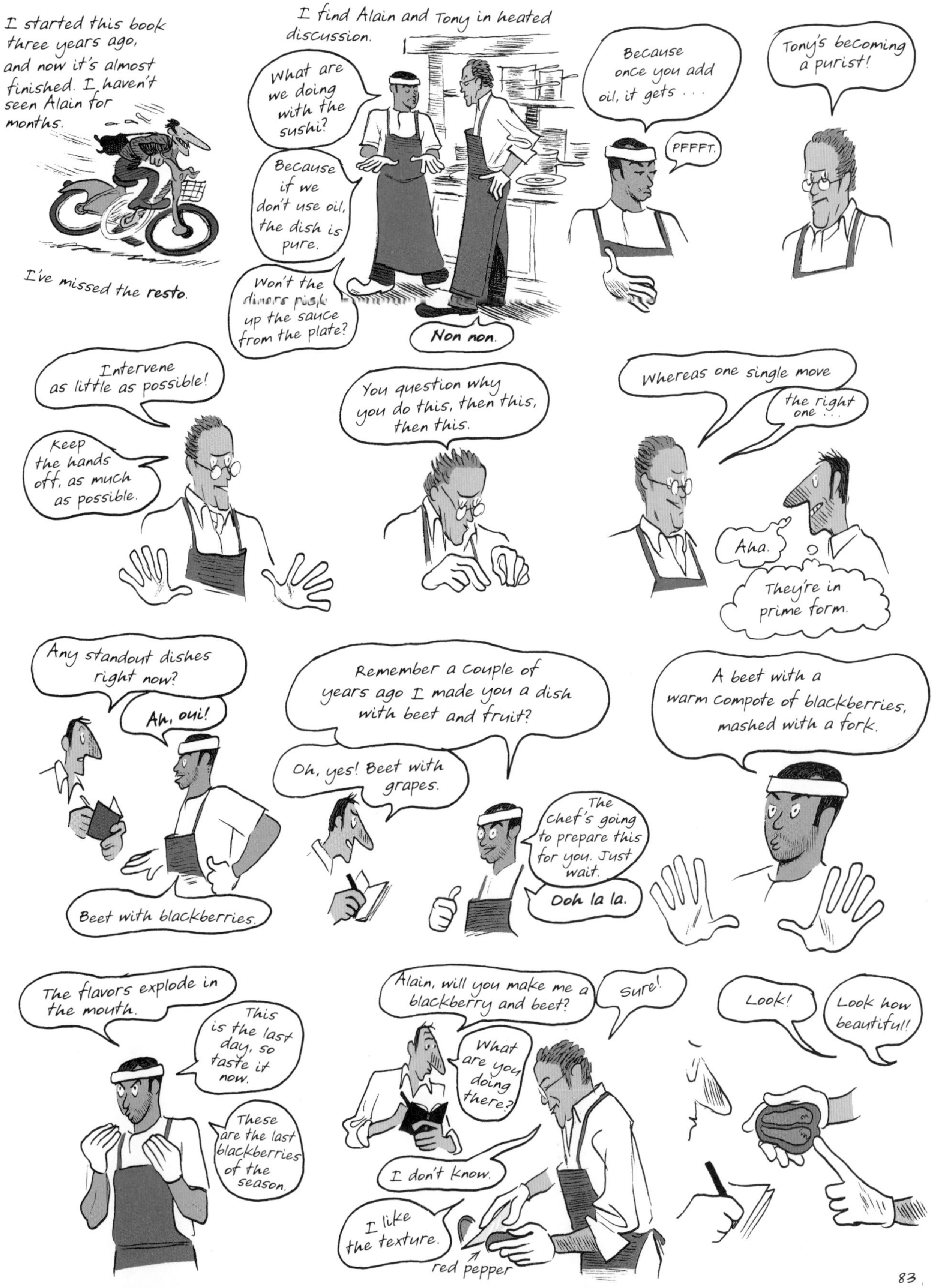

I started this book three years ago, and now it's almost finished. I haven't seen Alain for months.
I've missed the **resto**.
I find Alain and Tony in heated discussion.
What are we doing with the sushi?
Because if we don't use oil, the dish is pure.
Won't the diners pick up the sauce from the plate?
Non non.
Because once you add oil, it gets . . .
PFFFT.
Tony's becoming a purist!
Intervene as little as possible!
Keep the hands off, as much as possible.
You question why you do this, then this, then this.
Whereas one single move
the right one . . .
Aha.
They're in prime form.
Any standout dishes right now?
Ah, oui!
Beet with blackberries.
Remember a couple of years ago I made you a dish with beet and fruit?
Oh, yes! Beet with grapes.
The chef's going to prepare this for you. Just wait.
Ooh la la.
A beet with a warm compote of blackberries, mashed with a fork.
The flavors explode in the mouth.
This is the last day, so taste it now.
These are the last blackberries of the season.
Alain, will you make me a blackberry and beet?
Sure!
What are you doing there?
I don't know.
I like the texture.
red pepper
Look!
Look how beautiful!

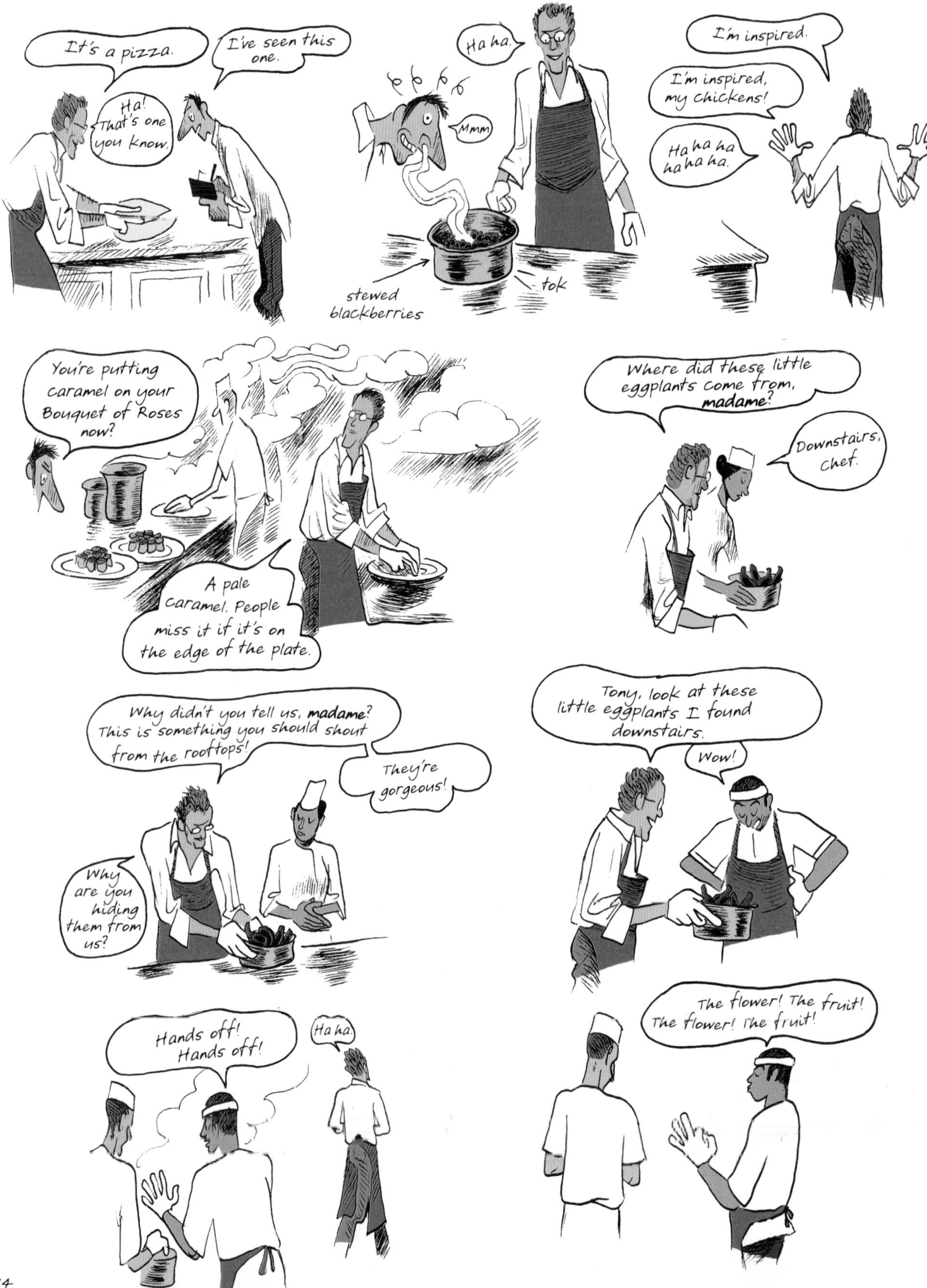
It's a pizza.
I've seen this one.
Ha! That's one you know.
Ha ha.
Mmm
stewed blackberries
tok
I'm inspired.
I'm inspired, my chickens!
Ha ha ha ha ha ha.
You're putting caramel on your Bouquet of Roses now?
A pale caramel. People miss it if it's on the edge of the plate.
Where did these little eggplants come from, **madame**?
Downstairs, Chef.
Why didn't you tell us, **madame**? This is something you should shout from the rooftops!
They're gorgeous!
Why are you hiding them from us?
Tony, look at these little eggplants I found downstairs.
Wow!
Hands off! Hands off!
Ha ha.
The flower! The fruit! The flower! The fruit!

Red Beet with Purple Basil and
Fork-Mashed Blackberries

▲▶◀◆◀▶▲▲

Vegetarian "Sushi"!

Red Beet with Purple Basil and Fork-Mashed Blackberries

SERVES 4

With a fork, mash 1 small bowl of freshly picked blackberries in a saucepan. Allow them to warm for 15 minutes over low heat. Add the leaves of 4 sprigs of purple basil, 4 tablespoons of salted butter, and 2 tablespoons of soy sauce. While the blackberry-basil fondue simmers, boil 12 small spring beets, the size of ping-pong balls, in their skins, in salted water. Allow 20 minutes of cooking time. Drain them and let them cool for 10 minutes before removing the skin. Divide the blackberry fondue among four warmed plates, and place the half-warm beets on top. Sprinkle with fleur de sel and ring with foamed whole milk, made cappuccino style in an espresso machine.

To add to the purple-violet theme, you can sprinkle the plate with fresh lavender.

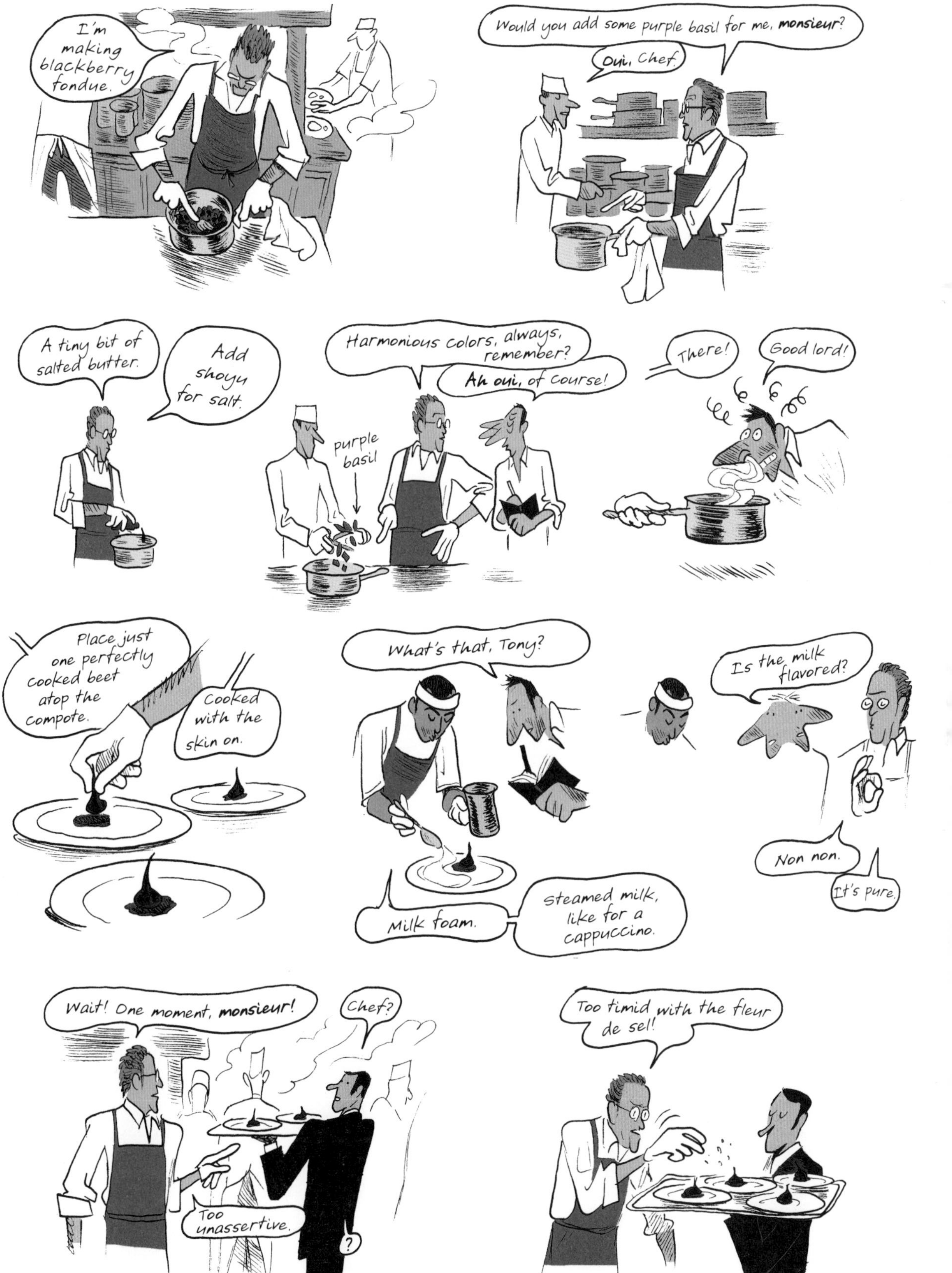
I'm making blackberry fondue.
Would you add some purple basil for me, monsieur?
Oui, Chef.
A tiny bit of salted butter.
Add shoyu for salt.
Harmonious colors, always, remember?
Ah oui, of course!
purple basil
There!
Good lord!
Place just one perfectly cooked beet atop the compote.
Cooked with the skin on.
What's that, Tony?
Milk foam.
Steamed milk, like for a cappuccino.
Is the milk flavored?
Non non.
It's pure.
Wait! One moment, monsieur!
Chef?
Too unassertive.
?
Too timid with the fleur de sel!

Vegetarian "Sushi"!

SERVES 4

Make a medley of diced vegetables: 1 carrot, 1 turnip, ½ small red cabbage, 1 small black radish, and 1 small fennel bulb. In a large bowl, mix this stuffing with ¼ cup plus 2 tablespoons of olive oil and 1 bunch of chives, finely chopped. Now place the stuffing on a round of rice paper, which has been soaked in cold water to soften it. Roll up the rice paper around the stuffing, creating a cylinder ½ inch in diameter. Make the sushi by cutting the roll into ¾-inch sections. Arrange them on a plate, and accent them with a squiggle of Orléans (or another French) mustard on the plate. Drizzle each sushi piece liberally with olive oil and soy sauce. Then top them with medallions of red, yellow, and ivory beets, alternating between them, all three steamed in their skins in salted simmering water.

To simplify the preparation, you can also julienne the vegetables.

I advise the smooth type of Orléans mustard, which is stone-ground; I love its brushed-gold color and meringuelike texture.

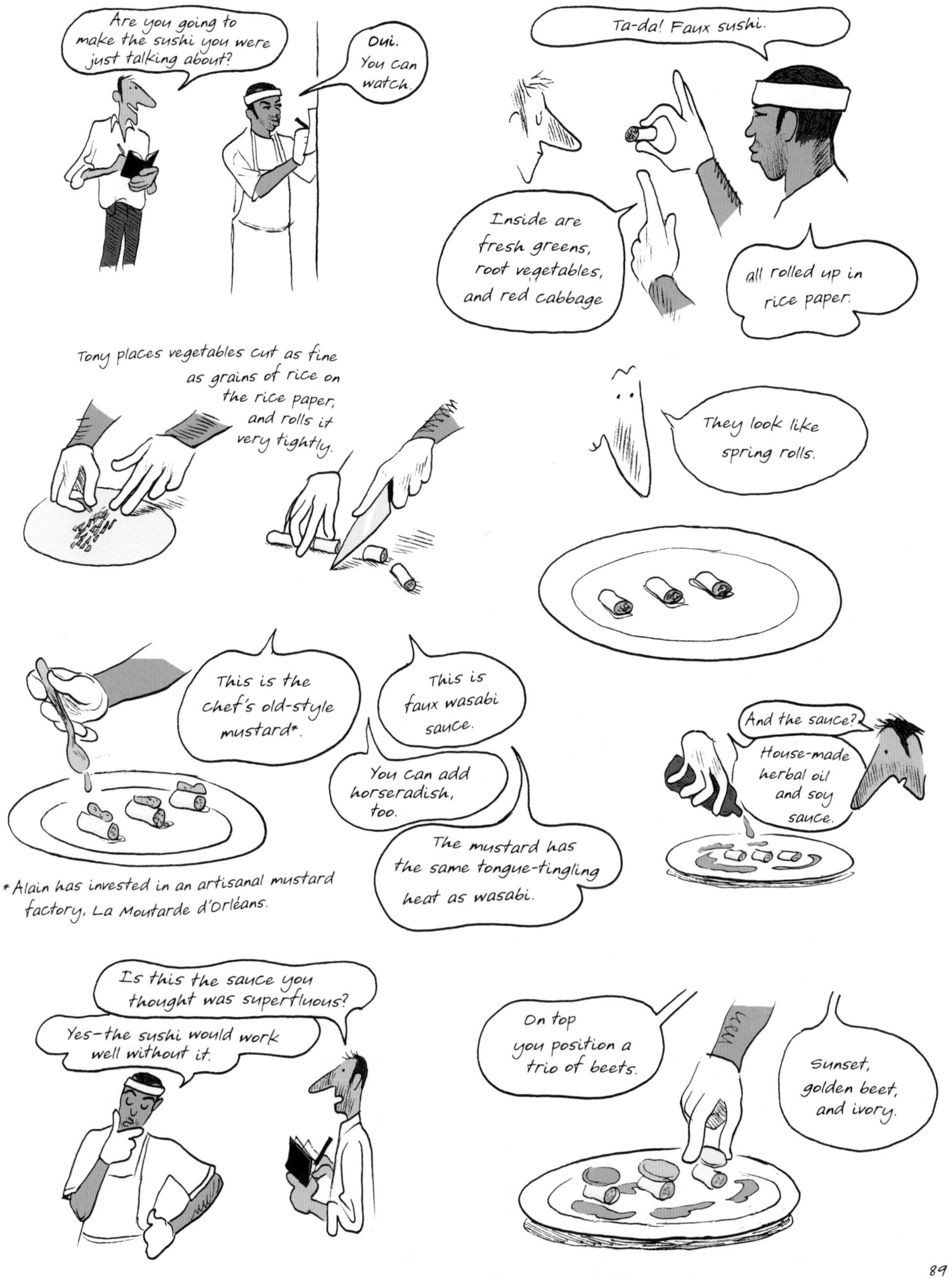
Are you going to make the sushi you were just talking about?
Oui. You can watch.
Ta-da! Faux sushi.
Inside are fresh greens, root vegetables, and red cabbage
all rolled up in rice paper.
Tony places vegetables cut as fine as grains of rice on the rice paper, and rolls it very tightly.
They look like spring rolls.
This is the chef's old-style mustard*.
This is faux wasabi sauce.
You can add horseradish, too.
The mustard has the same tongue-tingling heat as wasabi.
*Alain has invested in an artisanal mustard factory, La Moutarde d'Orléans.
And the sauce?
House-made herbal oil and soy sauce.
Is this the sauce you thought was superfluous?
Yes—the sushi would work well without it.
On top you position a trio of beets.
Sunset, golden beet, and ivory.

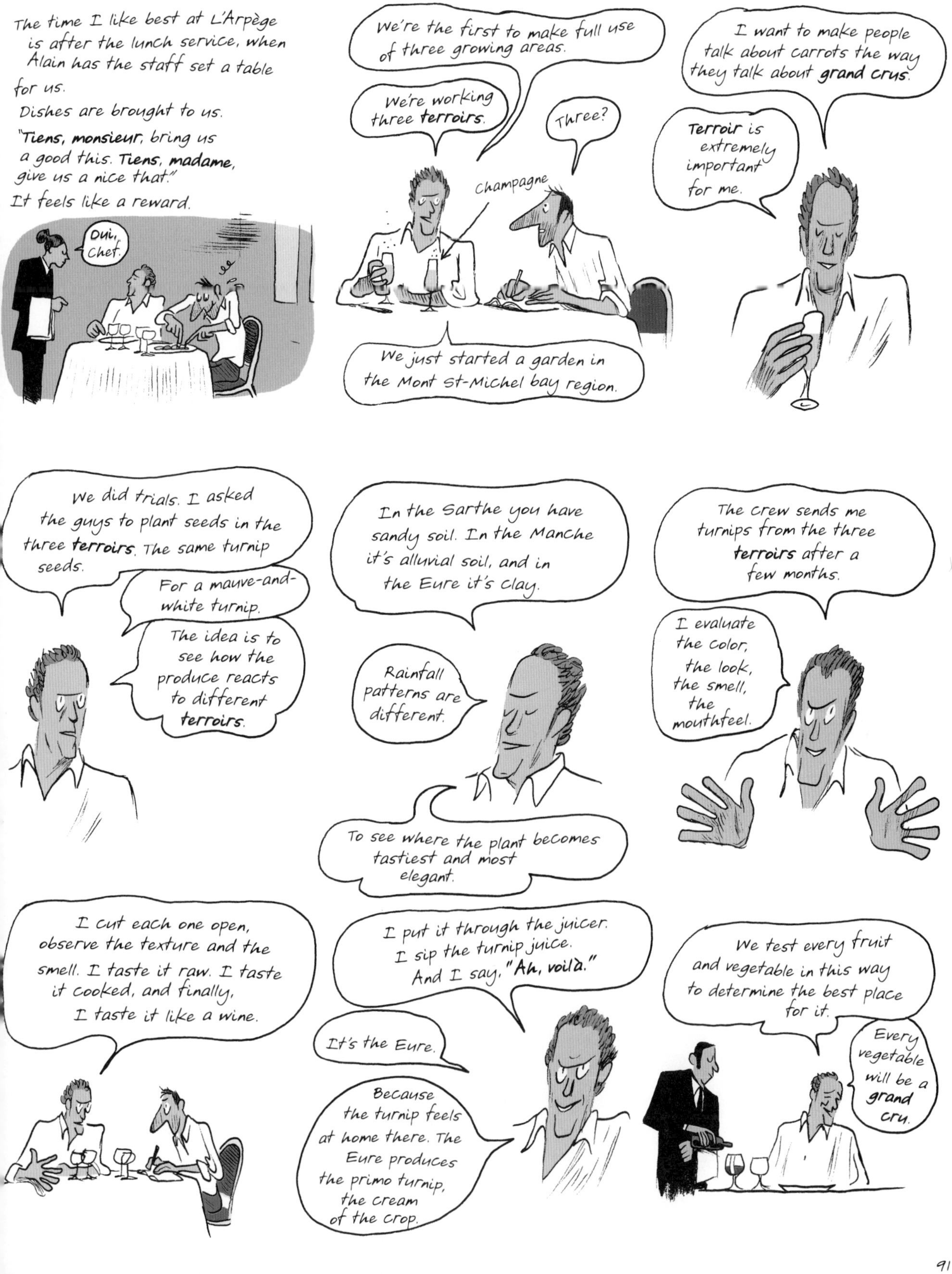
The time I like best at L'Arpège is after the lunch service, when Alain has the staff set a table for us.
Dishes are brought to us.
"**Tiens, monsieur**, bring us a good this. **Tiens, madame**, give us a nice that."
It feels like a reward.
Oui, Chef.
We're the first to make full use of three growing areas.
We're working three **terroirs**.
Three?
Champagne
We just started a garden in the Mont St-Michel bay region.
I want to make people talk about carrots the way they talk about **grand crus**.
Terroir is extremely important for me.
We did trials. I asked the guys to plant seeds in the three **terroirs**. The same turnip seeds.
For a mauve-and-white turnip.
The idea is to see how the produce reacts to different **terroirs**.
In the Sarthe you have sandy soil. In the Manche it's alluvial soil, and in the Eure it's clay.
Rainfall patterns are different.
To see where the plant becomes tastiest and most elegant.
The crew sends me turnips from the three **terroirs** after a few months.
I evaluate the color, the look, the smell, the mouthfeel.
I cut each one open, observe the texture and the smell. I taste it raw. I taste it cooked, and finally, I taste it like a wine.
I put it through the juicer. I sip the turnip juice. And I say, "**Ah, voilà.**"
It's the Eure.
Because the turnip feels at home there. The Eure produces the primo turnip, the cream of the crop.
We test every fruit and vegetable in this way to determine the best place for it.
Every vegetable will be a **grand cru**.

With Sylvain, our gardener in the Sarthe, it's all about tradition and grace.

He oversees the gardens.

Renaud, the gardener in the Eure, is more modern and extremely creative.

I'd like to make gardening the profession of the future.

Usually, gardeners don't taste what they grow.

My guys work with me on tasting.

I bought Renaud a smoker so he could smoke vegetables with different kinds of wood.

PUF PUF

Alain hands me his report on the turnip experiments. The look, the size, the olfactory trace of the **terroir** are all minutely detailed. Excerpt:

Raw Juice Extract—
Sarthe: Nose is bland, with unbalanced aromas. Juice light in color. In the mouth: first taste sensation, bitterness without elegance or grace. Nice aftertaste with slightly spicy finish.

Eure: Superb perfume, old-rose color. In the mouth: superb length, delicately astringent, bold, precise flavor.

Points (1-10)
Sarthe: 4
Manche: 6.5
Eure: 8

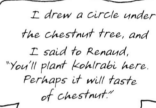

Right now we're working on the idea of producing "monocrop" compost.

For example, we have reeds that grow in our ponds.

Wouldn't they impart some freshness to our parsley?

We have a chestnut tree that has been giving compost to the soil every year, for sixty years now.

We're trying to understand the nature of the soil.

Its twigs, its leaves, its nuts.

I drew a circle under the chestnut tree, and I said to Renaud, "You'll plant kohlrabi here. Perhaps it will taste of chestnut."

We'll do the same thing under a fig tree, then with the other fruit trees.

Alain always bids farewell to his guests as they leave. He exchanges a few words with each one.

We go to his office on rue de Bourgogne.

Did you get a new motorcycle?

It's the same make.

I crashed the old one.

This evening I'm preparing a buffet dinner in Yvelines.

I'll have to jump on the cycle in my apron so I can get back to the restaurant right away.

Ha ha ha! What a circus!

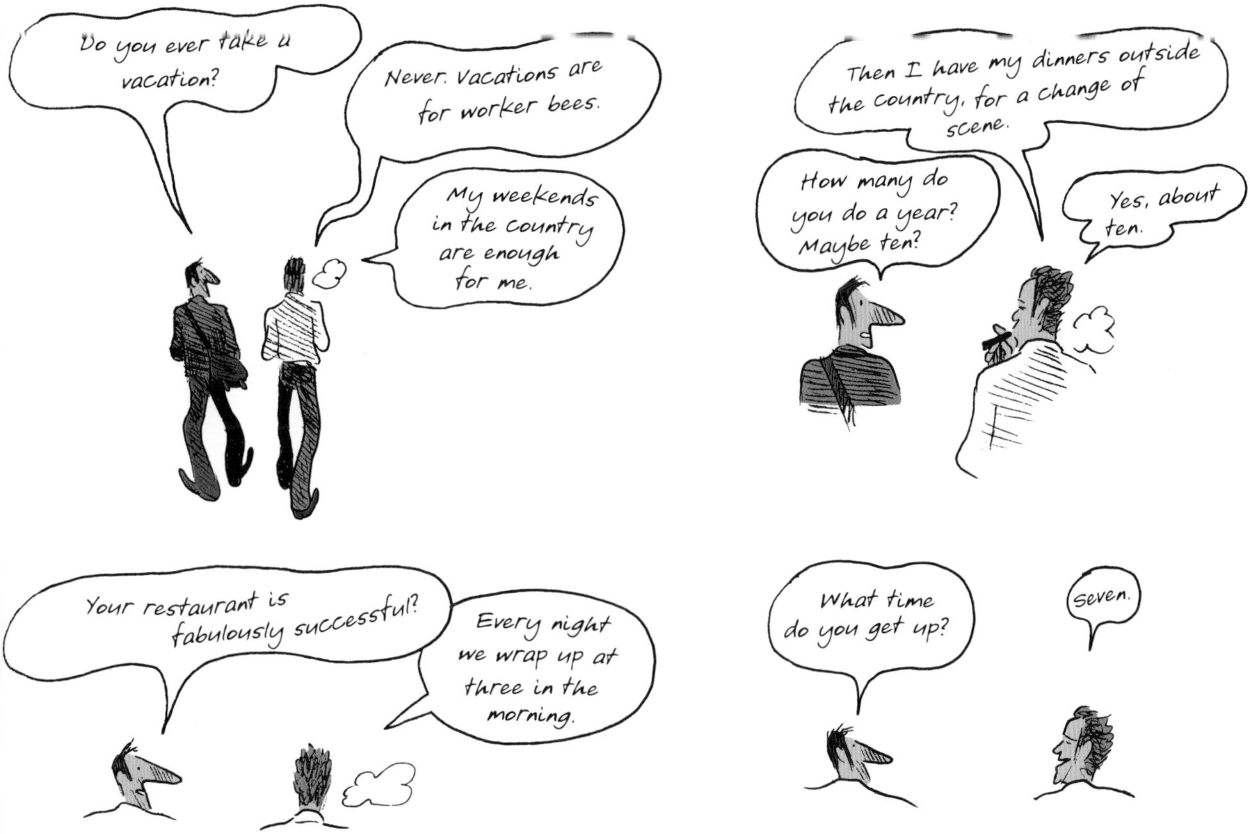
Do you ever take a vacation?
Never. Vacations are for worker bees.
My weekends in the country are enough for me.
Then I have my dinners outside the country, for a change of scene.
How many do you do a year? Maybe ten?
Yes, about ten.
Your restaurant is fabulously successful?
Every night we wrap up at three in the morning.
What time do you get up?
Seven.

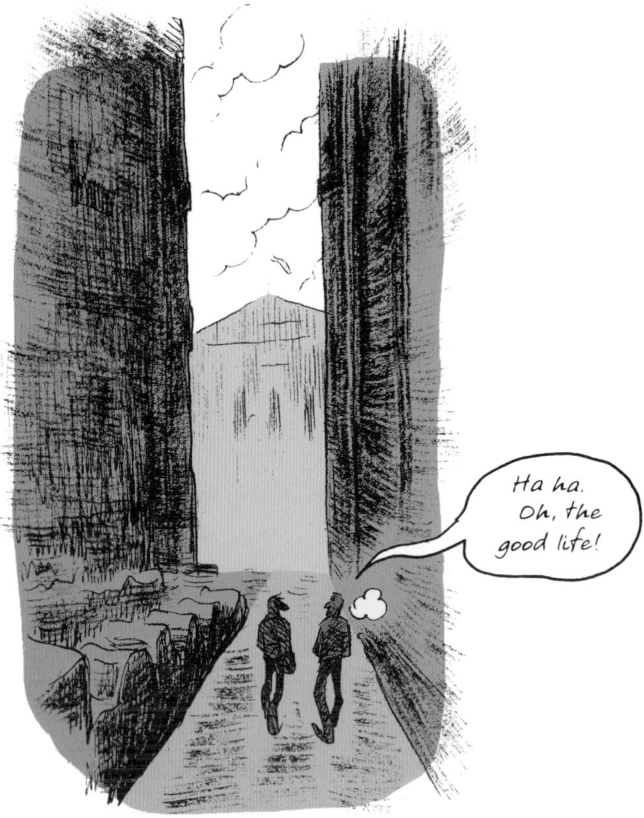
Ha ha. Oh, the good life!

Recipe Index